GW00326685

Charles_HRH's guide to

GREAT BRITISHNESS

Prince @Charles_HRH

headline

First published in Great Britain in 2014
by HEADLINE PUBLISHING GROUP

1

Cataloguing in Publication Data is available from the British Library

Hardback ISBN 978 1 4722 16267

Typeset in Century Oldstyle BT by
Palimpsest Book Production Ltd, Falkirk, Stirlingshire

Printed and bound in Great Britain by Clays Ltd, St Ives plc

Headline's policy is to use papers that are natural, renewable and
recyclable products and made from wood grown in sustainable forests.
The logging and manufacturing processes are expected to conform
to the environmental regulations of the country of origin.

HEADLINE PUBLISHING GROUP
An Hachette UK Company
338 Euston Road
London NW1 3BH

www.headline.co.uk
www.hachette.co.uk

CONTENTS

Dear Future Subjects

Firstly, one would like to congratulate you for making the right choice in purchasing a book written by a real member of the British Royal Family, and not Pippa Middleton, who recently released a book containing tips on entertaining guests throughout the British year. One's tip to you all: don't bother reading it.

The former Secretary of State for Education, Michael Gove, instructed all schools within the United Kingdom to 'promote the idea of Great Britishness'. Britain has a population of 63 million people with completely different perspectives on what this is, but we are all collectively united in what we think of Mr Gove.

When it comes to Great Britain, there is a vast amount of guidebooks available, but none have been given the all-important Royal Seal of Approval. Who better to teach the world about all things British than the man who just can't wait to be king, Prince @Charles_HRH?

One hopes this guidebook will become essential reading for tourists visiting Great Britain. Of course, one is aware of the dangers in making visitors too welcome in case they try and break into one's abode. There is simply nothing worse than having a lost soul of society extracted from the grounds of a royal residence on the end of a bayonet.

But this book is not just for our foreign visitors. Some of you might already happen to be British, but perhaps lack the finer details of Britishness that one needs to be a 100 per cent, fully fledged member of this distinguished nation. This is, of course, no fault of your own; one simply cannot help which social class one is born into. All other readers of this book are potential future subjects, should we decide to restore the Empire back to its former glory – this would be a damn sight easier if one had a spare afternoon between now and Christmas.

This book is your complete survival guide to the British Isles, featuring information and advice that has been ceremonially handed down through the ranks and generations of monarchy.

One is aware of these struggling times of financial crisis and a Coalition Government that is about as useful as a snooze button on a smoke alarm. As future subjects of oneself, this guidebook will help you deal with such troubles whilst making sure you're portraying the attributes of Great Britishness at all times.

Someone once said 'Everyone has a book inside them'. In some cases (Katie Price — twelve books and counting), that's exactly where the book should stay. But one thinks now is a good time to dust off the trusty quill pen, delve into the untouched archives of the monarchy and write one's first publication.

One hopes you all enjoy reading it.

Sincerely from your loving and ever graceful

Charles
(Future King)

How to Use this Book

1 Make sure the book is correctly positioned and that there are no obstacles in your line of sight.

2 Open the book. You are now ready to read, from left to right, one page at a time.

3 Once you have finished reading, close the book and place it where it can be found again by yourself or another member of the public, such as a table, public transport, staff canteen, teacher's desk, your local library or the House of Commons.

4 This book should *not* be used as a weapon, or a doorstop.

5 Please do not operate anything within this book if you're intoxicated with alcohol, as

all British etiquette and politeness becomes null and void; essentially you become European.

Welcome to Great Britain

It is a simple known fact that Great Britain is the most admired and envied country in the world. This little island is positioned in the centre of the globe and not round the arse end like Australia.

Britain gained the title 'great' from the rest of the world as they recognised Britain as their leader, as opposed to France, who were granted the unofficial title of 'failures' for losing more wars than every other country put together.

The British public is generally a modest, unassuming nation who seem to be obsessed with nothing more than the current weather. But beneath the façade is a resolute determination, confidence and pride that helped make the country the current undisputed World War Champion of the World.

To be born at all, is to be lucky; to be born British, is to have the winning ticket in the lottery of life. It's hardly surprising, then, that the British tend to feel sympathy for all the runners-up (the underdogs). In short, the best thing about being British is not being French. Or Russian.

Britain has made a great contribution to the modern world. After all, we did invent the steam engine, popular sports, the computer, America, mediocre pop music, the crumpet and the fine art of queueing.

For many, being British is about driving in a German car to an Irish pub for a Belgian beer, then getting an Indian takeaway or a Turkish kebab on the way home, to sit on Swedish furniture and watch American sitcoms on a Japanese TV, finished off with a moan about how the 'bloody foreigners ruined this great country'. And of course one is grateful for all our foreign chums' inventions. Personally one couldn't live without one's George Foreman grill.

Great Britain is a collection of three nations: England, Wales, Scotland* – we don't include Northern Ireland because it only causes trouble.

The English are British, and lots of people think the British are English, but that annoys the Scottish and Welsh, because although some think they're British and some think they aren't, and some think they are but don't want to be, they all agree that they are definitely not English. The Irish mostly think they are Irish, apart from the ones who are Northern Irish.

---

* One is writing this before the independence referendum 2014. If they vote 'yes' then every Scot will be gainfully employed – rebuilding Hadrian's Wall.

BRITISH EMPIRE

The **British Empire** (also known as the good old days) was an economic powerhouse in the early twentieth century when Britain ruled one-quarter of the world's population. Back in the day they were waiting for the next celestial alignment of the planets before crushing the remaining three-quarters and boldly invading where no country has stuck a flag before.

At the height of its influence, the British Empire was the most expansive colony the world had ever witnessed. Countries were invaded, occupied and made a little more like home; apart from the weather, obviously. The sun never sets on the British Empire, mainly because it's always bloody raining.

Of course, the Empire has been a major source of immigration to the UK; mostly via offering low-paid work by way of apology. Great Britain has benefited from the arrival of un-bland food that immigrants brought with them, along with a whole host of things that have enriched our culture, although Canada has been a bit lax in contribution, by only offering the 'music' of Justin Bieber.

The Empire has sadly declined from a quarter of the globe to a handful of twenty-two nations. Most countries were growing up fast and, like a teenager, wanted independence. The same happened on Harry's eighteenth birthday, when one made him promise not to go for a drink in Wetherspoons (unfortunately this rather backfired as he ended up in Spearmint Rhino ...).

The Empire officially ended in 1995 when the tourist-attraction sign at Junction 3 on the M3, which used to say 'Windsor. Royalty and Empire', was changed to 'Windsor. Legoland'.

THE COMMONWEALTH OF NATIONS

Formed from the ashes of the British Empire, the United Kingdom has a number of overseas dependencies known as the **Commonwealth** – so as not to confuse people between a great colonial expansion of a relatively small country and a crap magazine about films. These former colonies bring together trade and peace-keeping, along with a set of nations that we have some hope of beating at sporting events, and are now principally used for parking the Royal Navy.

THE UNION FLAG

The national flag of the United Kingdom, the **Union Flag**, often referred to as the Union Jack, is the greatest flag in the history of the world.

It was created in 1801 and is made up of three flags: the red cross of St George (England), the diagonal red cross of St Patrick (Northern

Ireland) and the white and blue saltire of St Andrew (Scotland). Obviously there should be a bloody great red dragon in the middle to represent Wales, but it was decided that one was enough to represent them.

The vibrant colours have become synonymous with Britishness. Prince Philip once joked that so many people have worn Union Jack boxer shorts over the years, the flag really should have a brown streak through the middle. That didn't go down too well during the inauguration of Australia celebrations.

CHAPTER 1

History of Great Britain

For some, history is that thing you hastily delete whilst logging off the Internet.

Unlike the United States of America, who fail to realise that there was actually life before 1492, the history of Great Britain is filled with triumphs and disasters and nearly as many wars as America has had in the last ten years. This being said, Great Britain should never be considered to be a warmongering country, as it's always someone else's fault.

As a general rule, if it happened prior to 1945 and it involved killing people, you can bet your Crown Jewels that Britain was involved.

This chapter contains scenes of violence, which some readers may find disturbing.

1066 – NORMAN CONQUEST

Great Britain has been invaded more times than one's had bacon sandwiches. Fortunately for us, every invader mysteriously became English when they took over, thus leaving England undefeated. This was particularly lucky in the year 1066, when the bloody French won their first (and last) war against England.

The **Battle of Hastings** is the only blemish on an otherwise spotless record of military supremacy. Many historians have described it as the worst defeat ever for the English, although they clearly haven't witnessed us playing a football match in the last forty years. The odd thing is that one isn't sure what Hastings was like in 1066, but it's certainly not worth fighting over now.

The invading Norman army was led by William the Conqueror, although he hadn't conquered anything then, so he was actually called William the Ugly Bastard. By middle age, he had become William the Fat Bastard.

During a quiet lull in battle, our ruler **King Harold II** was playing a quick game of I-spy, but failed to guess the 'something beginning with A' was actually a bloody sharp arrow fired by the Norman army that hit him directly in the eye. That'll teach him for leaving his glasses on the bedside table. He was severely wounded and, despite people telling him not to, he made it worse by frantically rubbing it, and died on the battlefield. He really should've gone to Specsavers.

Scenes from this battle are famously depicted on a 4½-mile long scarf, knitted by sexually frustrated French art students five years after the battle took place, and is on display in Bayeux, France.

1215 – MAGNA CARTA

The **Magna Carta** (Great Charter) is the most famous and significant legal document in history. **King John** wasn't popular amongst British society in 1215. To avoid potential rebellions, English barons provided him with the world's first Dear John letter listing his many faults.

The King reluctantly signed the document, which granted certain rules, rights and regulations to monarchy, servants, peasants, farmers and slaves including:

- The common rights of men.

- The power to piss off the French.

- Dress-down Fridays.

- Limiting royal duties to opening buildings and waving at sporting events.

Unfortunately for the generations to come, someone spilled their drink over the rule that banned the making of painfully bad films about Robin Hood.

Every British person should roughly know where the most important document in British history, the Magna Carta, was signed.*

King John's humbling defeat centuries ago seems unimaginably distant; a weak leader who'd risen to the top after betraying his brother, compelled by a group of unruly barons to sign on the dotted line. Although it is perhaps something the Miliband brothers know a thing or two about.

1605 – GUY FAWKES AND THE GUNPOWDER PLOT

 MPs want an 11 per cent pay rise?! Someone get Guy Fawkes on the phone.

* At the bottom.

In 1605, **Guy Fawkes** and his Catholic revolutionaries plotted to blow up King James I during the Opening of Parliament, mainly because he was a Protestant, and Scottish. However, some of the conspirators were concerned about fellow Catholics who would be present at Parliament during the opening. One of them wrote an anonymous letter to Lord Monteagle, warning him about the attack. Despite the coded vagueness of the warning, Lord Monteagle was made highly suspicious by the words 'We're going to blow up the King and everyone else during the State Opening of Parliament' and the plot was foiled.

Guy Fawkes was captured in the cellar, surrounded by thirty-six barrels of gunpowder and ten packets of multicoloured sparklers, with a match in one hand, trying to convince everyone that he'd just come to check the underground plumbing. It may have been Fawkes's military occupation that gave away his intentions to the palace guards, though his 'asking for a light' is certainly thought to have alerted them.

After being subjected to continuous singing by the Cheryl Cole equivalent of 1606, he confessed his sins. Found guilty, he was hung, drawn and quartered at Westminster; the penalty at the time for high treason prior to ASBOs.

Guy Fawkes's reputation has undergone improvement and today he is often toasted as 'The last man to enter Parliament with honest intentions'. If this were to happen today, he would receive a knighthood.

The British public has become fond of the **Gunpowder Plot** and it is celebrated on 5 November, **Bonfire Night.** This is the one night of the year when the whole of the UK comes together with bonfires and fireworks in commemoration of the last time the British Government actually found weapons of mass destruction. There really is no better way for Britain to recover from recession than burning millions of pounds' worth of fireworks at Westminster, although one isn't entirely sure if the yearly celebrations are for Guy Fawkes getting caught, or at least having a go.

Bonfire Night Safety Tips

1 Be very careful when transporting your fireworks. Especially if you're moving thirty-six barrels of highly explosive gunpowder into the cellars below the Houses of Parliament.

2 Stand well back when lighting fireworks bought from UK supermarkets, preferably 3 miles.

3 When throwing the guy on a bonfire, always make sure it isn't actually a sleeping member of UKIP.

4　Simulate the thrill of having your own dazzling display without spending a fortune by looking at the sky and watching other people's fireworks.

5　Never use fireworks in or around Dover, as France may see this as an act of war and surrender immediately, which could cause a lot of paperwork.

1665–6 – GREAT PLAGUE OF LONDON

The **Great Plague of London** was the last epidemic of the bubonic plague; a highly infectious disease, but nowhere near as harmful as the newly discovered Bieber Fever, which can be fatal to young adolescent girls.

The outbreak of the disease is thought to have been transmitted through the bite of an infected rat flea. The other, more controversial theory, suggests that the French were to blame; whereas another theory also blames the French.

The plague was responsible for the death of approximately 100,000 Londoners, all of whom contracted it on the Northern line, still coloured black on the Underground map as a warning from our history.

1666 — GREAT FIRE OF LONDON

The **Great Fire of London** was a large, destructive fire that swept through the city causing a considerable amount of civic improvement. Though extremely tragic for the city's occupants, it remains one of the only times the capital has ever reached a temperature over 30 degrees Celsius.

In the early hours of the morning on Sunday 2 September 1666, **Thomas Farynor**, the owner of Greggs the Bakery, Pudding Lane, was awoken by his wife:

'Honeybunch, did you turn the oven off?'

'No, the jumbo sausage rolls are still cooking.'

'Oh, Tom, you know the new rules about leaving the oven on unattended.'

'Health and safety gone mad. What's the worst that can happen?'

Before long flames were spreading through the entire building and the couple escaped over the rooftops. Sadly they left behind Kipper the dachshund, who became the first casualty in the Great Fire of London, but ultimately his demise led to the accidental invention of the world's first hotdog.

The blazing inferno spread to surrounding buildings and to his irritation the Mayor of London (Boris Johnson's great-great-great-great-great-great-great-grandfather) was immediately woken up. He looked out of his window and famously uttered 'A woman might piss it out', then went back to his beauty sleep. Whether this was actually attempted is not recorded.

According to the bakery owner, it was a complete accident, despite the fact most locals considered him to be a liar, liar, pants on fire type of person. Literally.

The fire lasted for 5 days, destroying 44 brothels, 17 underwear boutiques, 12 dental surgeries, 7 Nando's, 4 KFCs and some other unimportant buildings too.

Today, the site of the start of the fire is marked by the **Monument**, a 200-foot tower, topped with a gilded urn, representing a cream bun.

1805 – BATTLE OF TRAFALGAR

Horatio Nelson was Great Britain's greatest naval hero who beat the French, Spanish and

Danish fleets and still had enough energy to grapple with his mistress, Emma Hamilton, on his days off.

The French and Spanish prepared an invasion fleet of 33 ships, with 14,000 crew. During their voyage they met face to face with the greatest defence to ever exist: the British weather.

Nelson is commemorated in London's **Trafalgar Square** with **Nelson's Column**, which stands magnificently at 46 metres in the centre of the square. Originally, the four lions standing guard on each corner were real, right up to 1973, when they were stolen by Sir David Attenborough and replaced by statues. Upon the column's unveiling, in a fit of bravado and excitement, Nelson climbed up the column as part of a stunt. Unfortunately, with no clear way down, there he stayed.

1815 – BATTLE OF WATERLOO

The **Battle of Waterloo** is considered to be the greatest victory over the French, closely followed by Sir Bradley Wiggins's triumph in the Tour de France in 2012.

On 18 June 1815, a little after 2 p.m., the **Duke of Wellington** was just polishing off his ploughman's lunch, when Napoleon Bonaparte, a short French emperor who actually stopped growing at the age of nine, launched a surprise attack on Hougoumont Farm.

Wellington, who had intended to ride down to the farm and purchase some milk for his Earl Grey, was enraged to the point of using bad language (i.e. French). The French navy clearly failed to learn a valuable and important lesson the first time, ten years earlier at the Battle of Trafalgar: never come between an Englishman and his afternoon cup of tea.

On a boggy marshland outside of Waterloo, the Duke of Wellington chose his position carefully – a steep ridge that allowed his troops to peer down on the beautiful French women in the enemy camp. Somehow, this inspired the English to win the battle.

Maybe if Napoleon had chosen to rule a country with a higher success rate in winning things, he might have actually been victorious. Trust a Frenchman.

1939–45 SECOND WORLD WAR
Two World Wars, one World Cup, doo dah.

The **Second World War** was started due to Adolf Hitler's wish for world domination; something that One Direction are obsessed with today.

Hitler was clearly a nutcase from the very start, supported only by the forced German nation and the *Daily Mail*. Great Britain was on to him from the very beginning and made it clear that we wouldn't stand for his evil empire building and silly moustache. France signed up to the war thinking it was a six-year wine-tasting class, totally unaware of the dangers ahead.

Despite the best efforts of the von Trapp family, Britain declared war against Germany in 1939, but the French army, finally twigging what was going on, conveniently forgot how to fire their weapons. They bravely retreated to fight another day, except they also forgot to fight another day and were subsequently captured. It has to be said, though, that French engineers were innovators in building armoured vehicles. Each French tank was equipped with five gears; four to reverse out of battle and one going forward in case they were attacked from the rear.

Without help from anyone else, Great Britain was forced to single-handedly stop the advance

of the Nazis by using one of the most techno-
logically advanced defensive features of that
period: the English Channel. And try as they
might, the Germans were unable to break
Londoners' spirits during the Blitz. Good job
they didn't have a snow machine.

The war reached a climactic peak on 6 June
1944, when Allied forces landed on the shores
of Normandy. This event, known as D-Day,
marked the only time in history that the
British got to the beach before the Germans.

Eventually, with some reluctant help from the
USA and Russia, Great Britain brought the
Third Reich to its knees and liberated France
just as they finished learning the words to the
German national anthem. Not that they've
ever said thanks properly.

In April 1945, Hitler made his only sensible
decision of the war and committed suicide in
his bunker. Germany surrendered and took

little comfort in the famous **Winston Churchill** speech where he told them it wasn't the winning, but the taking part that counted.

Despite turning up late, the United States tried claiming victory, but due to the time difference between London and Washington, Great Britain had already claimed this several hours earlier.

CHAPTER 2

The Royal Family

Great Britain has come a long way since the days when ordinary folk were awestruck by aristocracy. One wouldn't want you to be fooled by the likes of *Downton Abbey*.

The Royal Family is one of many things that make Great Britain the greatest nation in the world. Being a member of the royals is just an accident of birth, something we all have to grin and bear.

Public interest in the British Royal Family is never-ending. Every detail of what we do, wear, eat and drink is passionately discussed on social media. The Royal Family is a soap opera to rival the absolute crap made by Channel 5. Our demands and popularity have dramatically risen in the past few years. We're so popular that the paparazzi are waiting around every corner for photographic opportunities of Harry airing his chopper. Sometimes one wonders what the British media would do without us.

The Royal Family has two main functions in modern Britain. The first is to cause friction amongst the social classes about what the 'bloody Royal Family' ever does for anyone. The second is to provide the tourist industry with ceremonial events, tea towels, commemorative mugs, postcards and other memorabilia. Camilla suggested 'a naked calendar to help give the economy a kick up the arse by overenthusiastic tourists', but everyone pretended they hadn't heard. Awkward.

Being a member of the British Royal Family means travelling everywhere in solid-gold transport, eating and drinking the finest food and wine, going on holidays 300 times a year and sitting through more Paul McCartney performances than is legally allowed.

A daily fly-on-the-wall-style update from
all royal palaces is currently being
planned, though obviously Prince Philip would
have to be locked away until after the
watershed.

It has been an interesting couple of years for
other worldly royals, with Queen Beatrix of
the Netherlands, the Emir of Qatar, Belgium's
King Albert II and the King of Spain all
stepping down from their thrones. Another
Juan bites the dust.

It's absolutely wonderful what some parents do
for their children.

THE CURRENT ROYALS
QUEEN ELIZABETH II
Born 21 April 1926
Mother, mama, mummy; constitutional head
of the United Kingdom and the
Commonwealth; wife to Prince Philip

Mother's a killer queen, guaranteed to blow
your mind.

Her Majesty has been on the throne for sixty-
two years, which means she'll be entitled to a
fantastic pension when/if she retires. Her
Diamond Jubilee was enjoyed by millions of
people around the world, including oneself.
The concert in the front garden of
Buckingham Palace was supposed to have
been the highlight of the weekend. One was
seriously glad of the pre-gig gin beforehand.
Not too sure what was more worrying – the
financial cost of it all or Cheryl Cole
attempting to sing. Camilla said the 'karaoke
contest sounded bloody awful' and that was
before Cliff Richard arrived on stage.

Father missed the whole event because he
was admitted to hospital with a bladder infec-
tion. That's honestly the last time one lets

him play drinking games. Although one suspects he deliberately did it to escape Elton John.

Many Paul McCartneys later, one ended the night with an epic speech regarding Mummy's sixty years on the throne. And if one doesn't mind saying so, one totally rocked the microphone.

Elizabeth and Philip have been married for nearly sixty-seven years, raising a family of four children and being blessed with eight grandchildren. The key to a long, healthy marriage is to make a solemn promise at the beginning: the first one to pack up and leave has to take all the children.

God save the Queen.

What's in the Queen's Handbag?

It's a question that has intrigued royal watchers for decades. The Queen has a collection of around 200 bags, some of them being 50 to 60 years old. She doesn't carry money, as it was assumed for many years that her own likeness would have the same effect as giving a dog a mirror and cause considerable confusion. People assume she doesn't need a British passport by law, but it's actually because she can't be arsed to drive all the way to Snappy Snaps for 'another sodding portrait'. Thankfully, no one has asked her for one yet.

Her Majesty's handbag contains:

- A portable hook. The hook is placed on the table's edge and used to secure the bag itself.

- Royal iPhone.

- Remote control for weapons. Only used in the emergency situation of a Middle Eastern dictator sodding about.

- Her current Prime Minister's left testicle.

- A tube of mints. Normally used when it's the Prime Minister's turn to speak during their weekly meetings.

- Crosswords. Used to let the Prime Minister know that he's beginning to sound like a stuck record.

- The Prime Minister's P45. Just in case.

- Miniature bottle of gin.

- Receipt for France.

PRINCE PHILIP, DUKE OF (HAZARD) EDINBURGH

Born 10 June 1941

Father; husband to Queen Elizabeth II

He is officially the highest-ranking racist in the country, despite the fact he could be considered an immigrant himself. He has perfected the art of saying hello and goodbye with a single handshake. As royal consort, forever at Mother's side, and often a few paces behind her, Father is renowned for his remarkable gift of politically incorrect gaffes. This could be put down to the fact that he's not in control of the Empire, his bladder or the nuclear button.

Here are some of Prince Philip's foot-in-mouth moments (allegedly):

'Well, you'll never fly in it, you're too fat to be an astronaut.'

– To a child, whilst visiting a space shuttle.

'You look like you're ready for bed!'

– To the President of Nigeria, who was wearing national dress.

'Ghastly.'

– Opinion of Beijing, China.

'How do you keep the natives off the booze long enough to pass the test?'

– To a Scottish driving instructor.

'You *are* a woman, aren't you?'

– To a Kenyan woman.

'Do you work in a strip club?'

– To a female sea cadet.

'Ah, you're the one who wrote the letter. So you can write then?'

– To a child, who invited the Queen to Romford, Essex.

'Ghastly.'

– Opinion of Stoke on Trent.

'Can you tell the difference between them?'

– To President Obama, who'd met with leaders of the UK, China and Russia.

CHARLES, PRINCE OF WALES
Born 14 November 1948
Future king

One is officially sixty-five years old. The idea of being able to retire before starting work seems strange, but something that one sadly has to accept. Being sixty-five means one is entitled to a free bus pass, though one has yet to figure out what it could be used for other than the weekly booze cruise to Threshers.

Her Majesty, Queen Elizabeth II, is gradually giving one more duties and responsibilities, which is a fancy way of putting 'Take the corgis out for a walk'.

After sixty-two years of being heir apparent to the throne, one decided it was time to join the twenty-first century and look into the realms of Twitter and Facebook. 'Charles likes this', although one has absolutely no intention of being poked, which would be the green light for all sorts of lewdness from Camilla. Social media is fast becoming the way that one can keep in touch with one's future subjects. Obviously, the easiest way would be to directly meet you all in person, but quite frankly that's unsafe, as one doesn't know where you've been.

One feels absolutely humbled and honoured to have won two prestigious awards: the Golden Twits Award 2012 in the Best Fake Celebrity category and a Shorty Award 2013 in the Best Fake Account category. It's almost as if they think one's Twitter account is a parody, which it clearly isn't. One simply cannot stand those silly things.

CAMILLA, DUCHESS OF CORNWALL
Born 17 July 1947
One's wife and lover

World's number one ABBA fan. Dinner with King Carl XVI Gustaf and Queen Silvia of Sweden proved to be a night to remember. Camilla decided to wear her bright-blue jumpsuit just to see the look on their faces. It must've taken them months to clean up the sequins. Just as one thought the night couldn't get any worse, the karaoke started. Camilla's song choice of 'Money, Money, Money' perhaps wasn't her greatest idea, considering the president of Greece was also sitting at our table.

Before Royal Ascot, one did consider sticking 'Number 7' on her back for a laugh, but decided against it. She might've become too excited by the prospect of being whipped by a stranger. That bloody book, *Fifty Shades of Grey*, has a lot to answer for.

It is an absolute certainty that she will say something without thinking it through first. One has lost count of the amount of times one is forced to smile, nod and carry on. During a royal visit to Wales, we stopped for an ice cream, where she accidentally asked for a 69. Awkward.

Besides her strange ways, Camilla is a very special human being. She is one's soulmate and equal, whom one loves dearly.

Well, someone's got to, haven't they?

PRINCE WILLIAM, DUKE OF CAMBRIDGE
Born 21 June 1982
Eldest son; father to Prince George

Prince William is a qualified RAF search-and-rescue pilot, recently married to Kate Middleton (you may have heard about it?). William broke with royal tradition and decided not to hire a stripper for his stag party, as it would've seemed strange stuffing pictures of his grandmother into her underwear.

Mr Cameron's Coalition Government met the news of an impending royal marriage with joy and jubilation:

Cameron: You heard the amazing news?!

Clegg: Oh my God, two for one at Papa John's!

Cameron: No, not that numbnuts, the royal wedding!

Clegg: Royal wedding? Posh and Becks are already married, aren't they?

Cameron: For Thatcher's sake, no. Prince William and Kate. This is exactly what we've been waiting for, as it will take the British people's minds off the recession and the fact they're losing their jobs.

Clegg: Fantastic news. This will be an especially joyous occasion in my house because we actually need new tea towels.

The stress of marriage and fatherhood has really taken its toll on William's heirline, which is showing more bald patches than the Centre Court at Wimbledon. But, thankfully, he's unfazed by it all, and says 'It's not baldness, it's a solar panel for a sex machine'.

KATE, DUCHESS OF CAMBRIDGE
Born 9 January 1982
Daughter-in-law; husband to Prince William;
mother to Prince George

As soon as one became aware of Prince William's interest in an outsider, one ordered a full genealogical survey of the Middleton family. When it came up with 'nothing known to embarrass' (yet), the Queen gave her official consent.

France caused a public stir in 2012, when they published photographs of Kate topless. Not entirely sure what all the fuss about Kate showing off her puppies was when we've seen loads of pictures of the Queen and her corgis.

Shortly after, royal doctors confirmed that Kate was suffering with an ingrown heir – a royal baby, which was growing a damn sight faster than the economy. The royal box was well and truly occupied.

No, Harry, you cannot help Kate. One doesn't care that 'morning sickness is often treated with ginger'.

It really is lovely to see how unfazed and undaunted Kate has become in performing royal duties. She has perfected the skilful art of waving and tweeting at the same time.

ROYAL WEDDING 2011

Nothing unites the nation more than a private **royal wedding** along the streets of London. It's the perfect excuse to have a party, drink huge amounts of alcohol and have a day off work. Millions of people around the world tuned in to watch William and Kate's nuptials on 29 April 2011. Just how many witnesses did one couple need, you may ask.

Several days before the big event, tents started to appear outside **Westminster Abbey**. On reflection, one should've paid for the Middleton family to stay in a hotel.

Royals from all over the world attended the ceremony. An unprecedented number of security staff were on duty, mainly to keep Harry away from the bridesmaids. William insisted on not having the traditional fruitcake at the wedding, but Father turned up regardless. That was awkward, but nothing compared to when the Archbishop of Canterbury raised his hand in order to give the final blessing at the end of the service and Kate totally misunderstood, giving him a high-five.

The day made headlines around the world, mainly due to record-breaking viewing figures and Pippa Middleton's posterior.

Royal wedding playlist:

- Abba – 'Dancing Queen'

- Blur – 'Bank Holiday'

- Adam and the Ants – 'Prince Charming'

- Kanye West – 'Gold Digger'

- Westlife – 'Queen of My Heart'

- Queen – 'Don't Stop Me Now'

- Pulp – 'Common People'

- Sex Pistols – 'God Save the Queen'

Wedding Gifts Received

- Mr and Mrs Middleton – 'luxury hamper' from Asda.

- King of Cyprus – his gift made it clear how bad their current financial situation is since becoming part of the EU. He didn't buy anything.

- Pope Benedict XVI – Vatican contraception, because blessed is he who comes in the name of the Lord. Awkward.

- Madonna – a six-month-old baby, which one gave straight back to the Immigration Service and Border Agency.

PRINCE GEORGE OF CAMBRIDGE
Born 22 July 2013
First grandson

On Her Majesty's Secret Cervix – the most important birth after Christ.

Nine months. Nine sodding months William and Kate had to wait for their half-blood prince. Quite frankly, that will be the last time they'll be using the NHS. One phoned the doctor at St Mary's Hospital early that morning to inform him that Kate was finally showing signs of giving birth. He became rather excited, as he'd be the first person in the world to see what stamps will look like in sixty years' time.

After much consideration about having a gin-induced labour, it was decided that a natural birth was the preferred choice. Kate wasn't too posh to push after all. The Queen and Prince

Philip had a private box next to the birthing suite; Pippa Middleton bent over by the bed to whisper words of encouragement into Kate's ear. For some reason Harry decided that was the time to start filming proceedings.

One decided to ignore the midwife who made a point of announcing 'The baby's crowning'. Kate was slightly alarmed when a baby started emerging with a golden halo around his head, as she hadn't been told royals are born with little crowns when they emerge from the royal box, hence the expression.

 Prince William's heir is falling out!

William burst into tears as he caught the first glimpse of his very own newborn baby. One couldn't decide if it was because his child will one day become king or because the baby had more hair than him. Poor sod.

Buckingham Palace was flooded with suggestions for a suitable name for the new baby. In keeping with a long-standing royal tradition, Prince Philip was asked to keep his opinions on this to himself.

One is pleased that William and Kate have a son, mainly because it means that Kate won't be beheaded. They have agreed that when the baby wakes in the night they will take it in turns to call the nanny. Harry is also happy about the arrival of the royal baby, simply because he won't be the only one running around the palace naked.

There is no truth to the rumour that the baby was presented on the balcony whilst the 'Circle of Life' was playing in the background. Sorry.

TOP SECRET – ONE'S LETTER TO PRINCE GEORGE

Dear Prince George Alexander Louis of Cambridge

Welcome to the British Royal Family. You kept the whole world waiting, but then that is one of the privileges. Many people would kill to become part of the monarchy, and they have done in the past. One day one will read you a bedtime story about Great-Uncle Henry Tudor and Great-Uncle Richard III when you're old enough to understand.

Royal blood is a highly prized commodity. It is so important that your ancestors used to marry within the family to keep the royal bloodline pure. However, this rule has been relaxed in the past couple of generations and one is certain that you'll get to know the Middleton family rather well in the coming years. They're a nice bunch really (in small doses).

By being born royal you've automatically quali-fied for certain perks of the job, including fabulous wealth, privileged lifestyle, a university placement and free unlimited downloads from iTunes. Soon you'll also be given your very own silver spoon. This will eventually be displayed outside Buckingham Palace to remind everyone that members of the British Royal Family are value for money.

Meet Your New Royal Family

Prince William and Kate (Mummy and Daddy) – Lovely couple. Don't be surprised to see that you've got more hair than your daddy. He wants to grow old gracefully.

Prince Harry (Uncle) – Well loved by everyone. Sometimes forgets he's a member of the Royal Family, which is why common people love him. Your arrival has bumped him down to fourth place in the royal line of succession, although one is certain we can avoid a 'Lion King situation'.

Prince Charles and Camilla (Grandpa and Step-nanny) — Grandpa just can't wait to be king, but that's our little secret. Nanny Camilla has been busily knitting you some clothes, as another naked royal in the newspapers is the last thing one needs.

Queen Elizabeth II and Prince Philip (Great-nanny and Great-grandad) — An old married couple. Great-nanny wears a crown covered in jewels, which might look like a giant Iced Gem to you. She is obsessed with corgis, horses, gin and ridiculous hats. Great-grandad might come across as slightly racist and rude, but just smile and nod. Most people do.

The Rules of Royalty

1 Everything the light touches is our kingdom. Except the shadowy place, that's Essex.

2 The British Empire ended in 1997, but don't tell the rest of the world. It keeps them all in check.

3 You should never be referred to as 'Boy George', simply because you are a future king, and not a queen.

4 Never, under any circumstances, take fashion advice from Beatrice and Eugenie.

5 Don't listen to music by Justin Bieber or One Direction, purely because it's an act of treason.

6 Stay away from Las Vegas.

One day in the future, when Grandpa and Daddy are pushing up daisies, you will: be crowned king of 16 sovereign states, be head of the 53-member Commonwealth of Nations, be a gold member of the Sony PlayStation Network, have reached the highest prestige level of Call of Duty and be Supreme Governor of the Church of England, Lord of the Rings and Defender of the Faith.

One wishes you good health and a happy life.

Love always

Grandpa @*Charles_HRH*
(Future King)

HARRY, PRINCE HENRY OF WALES
Born 15 September 1984
Youngest son; wild child; a fun-loving person who occasionally lets his hair (and trousers) down.

Earned a reputation in his youth for being rebellious when he attended a party dressed in a Nazi uniform. That certainly was the last time one allowed him to borrow a costume from Prince Michael of Kent's wardrobe.

In 2012 he was photographed naked whilst on holiday in Las Vegas, which was the last thing one expected to see splashed all over the media. That morning one had coincidentally sent Camilla to the shop for a packet of ginger nuts and she returned with the *Sun* newspaper. Nearly choked to death on one's sausage sandwich.

 No, Harry, we cannot 'pretend it was Ed Sheeran'.

It seems he totally misunderstood his invitation to 'hang out'. There is only one set of Crown Jewels that should be seen in public and they're made from diamonds. Harry thinks the girl who sold the nude photographs to the press was 'despicable', which seems a strange name for a Vegas stripper.

ANNE, PRINCESS ROYAL
Born 15 August 1950
Sister

ZARA PHILLIPS
Born 15 May 1981
Niece

In an effort to promote a normal life, it was decided by her mother, Anne, that Zara would not bear the title of princess. This had the unfortunate side effect of making reading fairy tales to the young royal quite a challenge.

Zara met Mike Tindall whilst attending the Rugby World Cup in Australia in 2003, which England would go on to win. It is every man's dream to one day meet his princess and have a big wedding in a huge church, with the eyes of the nation gazing admiringly upon them. But considering the cost of William and Kate's wedding earlier in 2011, they had to have it in a low-key registry office instead. Awkward.

The happy couple were delighted to receive their first minor royal baby on 17 January 2014 when Mia Grace was born, complete with large dodgy ears and a wonky nose. Although she has also inherited some features from Mike Tindall.

PRINCE ANDREW, DUKE OF YORK
Born 19 February 1960
Brother

Andrew is known for leading a life of eating, drinking, playing golf, marrying redheaded hockey girls and generally living like a patron saint. He has had many ups and downs in the past couple of years, but then that would have something to do with being the Duke of York.

Recently, he was challenged by police in the gardens of Buckingham Palace and officially asked to identify himself. You can't really blame them, as they are specially trained in recognising all *active* members of the Royal Family. The grand old Duke of York, he had ten thousand men. But two of those men were unfamiliar with his appearance, so they marched him off again.

His ex-wife Sarah Ferguson has gone on record to say she was drunk when she agreed to sell access for cash, and Prince Andrew wants it to be known he was drunk when he married her.

PRINCESSES BEATRICE AND EUGENIE
Born 8 August 1988 and 23 March 1990 respectively
Nieces.

When Andrew's daughters, Beatrice and Eugenie, emerged from the car with their questionable hats at the royal wedding, there was a rather polite silence, broken only by the sound of a fatal fashion error dropping on the ground. One's initial thought was 'Where's Cinderella?' The hats were placed on eBay afterwards, where one received a grand total of £7.28p. Unfortunately the highest bidder thought they were actually buying indoor aerials and spent most of an afternoon trying to pick up ITV.

PRINCE EDWARD
Born 10 March 1964
Brother

Edward is the youngest, overlooked and forgotten member of the royal litter, often mistaken for a reflection or a strong gust of wind. He must sometimes feel like the fourth man on the moon, the one no one's heard of; or that fellow from Wham, who used to sing alongside George Michael.

Royal Fun Facts

- Queen Elizabeth II has impersonated a number of famous people and recently won an Academy Award for her interpretation of Helen Mirren in the film *The Actress*.

- Prince Harry loves playing games with the Royal Family, especially at Christmas. His favourite is charades, although his interpretation of *Free Willy* is totally inappropriate.

- One told Camilla not to buy anything expensive for one's sixty-fifth birthday, so she bought Spain. It's the thought that counts.

- Prince Harry is commonly known in the British Army as Private Parts.

- Queen Elizabeth II owns all swans, is saved daily by God, can believe it's not butter, doesn't pay too much for her car insurance and hasn't been involved in an accident that wasn't her fault.

- There is no truth to the rumour that Edward and oneself had a hit in 1992 with 'Would I Lie to You?'

The Middleton Family

The **Middletons** are simply overjoyed that their genes have contributed to the future of the monarchy. How lovely.

Carole and Michael Middleton own a party-supplies company. Their sales and profits rose dramatically during the Diamond Jubilee as 'the whole of England went absolutely bunting mad'. At least one thinks that's what they said.

Pippa Middleton, Kate's sister, has written many books, columns and other little obscurities since showing prominence at the royal wedding. Her now-famous posterior has unwittingly forced her to become the butt of every royal joke.

ROYAL HOUSEHOLDS
BUCKINGHAM PALACE

Buckingham Palace is the main royal residence where Queen Elizabeth II and Prince Philip are kept.

The most famous part of the palace is the balcony, which is used for photo opportunities and Camilla's cheeky fags. The Royal Air Force proceeds with a flypast over Buckingham Palace during important engagements, but due to recent budget restraints they'll be using the easyJet route from Luton to Barcelona.

The master bedroom is where the magic regularly happens. One seriously regrets buying Camilla the wizardry starter kit from the Harry Potter studios.

There are three ways to visit Buckingham Palace:

1 Purchase a ticket from various tour guides.

2 Become a Sir or a Dame.

3 Break in, which is extremely foolish unless you're willing to have a corgi's tooth surgically removed from your arse cheek.

Clad in their distinctive red tunics and bear-skin hats, the soldiers of the **Queen's Guard** are charged with protecting official royal residences and have been proven to be far more effective than a spyhole and doorbell. Guidelines are in place for guards to deal with public nuisances and Members of Parliament, which begins with stamping their feet and shouting. If that doesn't work then they point a fixed bayonet directly at the person's chest – something that has a surprisingly high success rate at calming an aggressive person.

Queen Elizabeth II is notorious for being easily bored and regularly screams 'Won't someone change this bloody guard?' out of the window most mornings. It's a little known fact that if you can knock off the furry hats of three Queen's Guards, you win a coconut. Make him laugh and he'll give you £20.

Buckingham Palace officials were heavily criticised during the Diamond Jubilee as people were concerned that the red, white and blue of the Union Jack being projected on to the palace looked remotely like the national flag of France. One thought this was strange, as one always assumed the French flag is white.

The Royal Standard of the United Kingdom is flown to signify that members of the Royal Family are at home. The original purpose of this custom was to advertise that anyone who fancied a chat was welcome to nip up to the front gates and request an audience. In modern times, the flag flown high above the residence serves as a signal to the milkman to leave six pints of milk if the Royal Family is home and four pints if they are not.

THE TOWER OF LONDON

The **Tower of London** was built in 1078 by William the Conqueror (not literally, he sat watching). It was primarily a royal residence, but is now better known as a prison for those who have committed treason and dodgy celebrities such as Sir Paul McCartney, who has been imprisoned since the Diamond Jubilee. His public performances of 'Hey Jude' sixteen times in the space of a year were frankly criminal and one had to act.

Several members of the British Royal Family have also been imprisoned there, including **Henry VI, Elizabeth I** and the **princes in the tower,** who were supposedly slaughtered – William on vodka and Red Bull and Harry on rum and Coke.

Prisoners would be subject to physical and psychological torture. Methods included bone breaking, castration, dunking, starvation, disfigurement, boiling, sleep deprivation, scalping and Justin Bieber's music on loop.

The tower hasn't only housed royalty and prisoners. It's been used as the Treasury, an armoury, the Royal Mint, a public records office, Mr Clegg's nursery and to house the Crown Jewels (no, not like that Las Vegas hotel room, Harry). It has also been used as a menagerie, which housed an array of animals including elephants, polar bears, lions and other beasts from the jungle, including the winners of *I'm a Celebrity*.

There are normally seven ravens that live at the tower. The presence of these birds is due to the tradition that they were believed to protect the Crown and the tower; a superstition holds that 'If the ravens leave the tower, the Crown will fall and Britain with it'. So,

please don't sod around or they'll peck your
eyes out.

The only other types of birds kept at the
tower are to do with Prince Harry, but one
doesn't have time to dwell. Another time
perhaps.

PREVIOUS MONARCHS
RICHARD III (B. 1452 D. 1485)

Richard had been the ugly runt in the family.
Whereas his brother Edward IV had good
looks, he had a large hump on his back. After
receiving no reply to several letters sent to
Quasimodo in Notre Dame to apply for the
position of assistant bell ringer, Richard hung
about in the hope that something would come
his way.

Edward had provoked criticism by marrying
Elizabeth Woodville, a widow and commoner.
After his death, an assembly of nobles declared
his marriage illegal, and his sons – the young

King and his brother – illegitimate. Richard seized the crown for himself, and the princes, who had been staying in the Travelodge Tower of London, were never seen again.

Richard's reign survived a rising in 1483, but Henry Tudor's invasion in 1485 ended in his death.

Might have to sell France to pay for Richard III's car-park fine.

Now is the winter of our discovery in cement. In 2012, a team of excavators discovered the remains of Richard III under a car park in Leicester. Apparently he died there when the Royal Horse Association failed to find him a replacement stallion when his original broke down in the mud at the Battle of Bosworth Field. After declaring Richard's skeleton the Hide 'n' Seek Champion of 1485, closer examination concluded that the curvature of his spine was not due to scoliosis, but merely caused by turning in his grave after seeing what Leicester has become.

The newly discovered remains of monarchy has forced one to completely renew the royal edition of Cluedo: Henry V, in the car park, with a shovel.

Following the discovery, archaeologists are now digging up Tesco's car park looking for the remains of his horse.

KING HENRY VIII (B. 1491 D. 1547)
Henry was an irritable, foul-tempered, nasty brute with ginger hair and a horrid beard, who was most famous for having six wives, whose sequence of fate goes thus: divorced, beheaded, died, divorced, beheaded, survived. Not really a track record that would make him worth a punt if you saw his profile on a dating website. He ruled over the entire kingdom of England and was a dedicated

sportsman in his youth, though he let himself go when he got married, as all British men do.

Six marriages gave him three children; one son and heir, and two girls, which back during the Tudor period were considered less important than owning a decent suit of armour. Henry blamed everyone for his poor breeding record and executed anyone who would dare to mention it.

QUEEN ELIZABETH I (B. 1533 D. 1603)

Queen Elizabeth I may have had the body of a weak and feeble woman but she had the heart and stomach of a king, which she kept in a pickle jar on her mantelpiece.

Elizabeth never married. This was partly because of men's pathetic 'I'm the boss' insecurities and partly because she didn't need a husband dawdling in the background, getting in the way during state business, only ever expressing an opinion in the hope that they'll stop being asked questions and then get to go home.

Her leadership, intelligence, murderous rage and fashion sense are proof that only a woman can be trusted to run a country properly; according to Mother anyway.

KING GEORGE III (B. 1738 D. 1820)
King George III is best known for being nutty as a fruitcake. His madness meant he couldn't rule a sentence, never mind a country.

His acts of insanity included ending every sentence with the word 'peacock', which is three letters more than Mr Cameron's nick-name within the royal household.

George managed to lose the American colo-nies, which were granted independence on 4 July 1776 – the day the average IQ of the

British Empire jumped 100 points with a single signature. In America, this is classed as a victory, but the British see it as a lucky escape, simply because we couldn't be arsed with them anymore.

The Madness of King George III is a fantastic film in which Nigel Hawthorne gives a very accurate portrayal of the king. American audiences didn't go to see it because they hadn't seen the first two. Awkward.

QUEEN VICTORIA (B. 1819 D. 1901)
The famously stony-faced monarch, who reigned for sixty-three years and seven months, oversaw Britain's birth as a fish-and-chip industrial nation. As was traditional with so many monarchs, **Queen Victoria** was named after a pub in Albert Square, Walford.

Unable to find a man suitable for herself in the British Empire, Victoria's ministers were dispatched to Germany, where they discovered her first cousin, **Prince Albert of Saxe-Coburg and Gotha**. Following in a tradition that has kept European monarchy in pure blood and extra toes for the last 400 years, she became known as the 'Grandmother of Europe', as she eventually gave birth to half of Europe's royals.

Every corgi has its day, and every reign had a name. Queen Victoria cleverly settled on the Victorian Era. She took the British Empire to its ultimate peak and into the modern age, witnessing the start and growth of the railway, and the first instance of leaves on the line at King's Cross St Pancras.

KING GEORGE VI (B. 1895 D. 1952)
King George VI was reluctantly crowned after his elder brother, Edward VIII, abdicated to marry an American divorcee, Ms Wallis Simpson, who quite rightly pointed out, 'You can't abdicate and eat it.'

George's life was depicted in the fascinating film *The King's Speech*, although one is slightly bemused that Colin Firth won the Academy Award for Best Actor considering he could barely remember his lines.

CHAPTER 3

Government

Government — a group of people that exist for the purposes of increasing debt, widening the gap between the rich and poor, and funding world domination projects such as Europe. Governments tend not to solve problems, only to rearrange them.

The Houses of Parliament is the only waxwork museum in the world in which the exhibits are in charge. They are responsible for convincing the population of the United Kingdom that they run the country, which they don't.

Members of Parliament are a major source of entertainment across the globe. MPs spend most of their time drinking tea, chatting about how idiotic the Mayor of London is, guessing how much money they each earn, claiming expenses and working out who has the closest connection to oneself and other royalty.

It is considered rude not to insult your fellow members. Politeness amongst ministers is extremely bad form. Proper conduct requires that members must be insulted in direct proportion to their power and position at least once a week.

Elections are generally held every five years, though it doesn't really matter who you vote for, as everyone knows the Queen decides anyway. Old-style general elections are soon to be replaced by weekly phone votes to evict unpopular housemates.

Although not a direct insult, Margaret Thatcher is used as a yardstick to test public hatred for politicians. Gaining a 60 per cent Maggie Rating is 'the greatest accomplishment' for even the most liked politician.

Yes Minister

This is a documentary about the British Civil Service and a Cabinet minister, broadcast on BBC2 between 1980–84. Due to an editing error, canned laughter was added to the documentaries making audiences believe, even to this day, that it was meant to be a comedy series.

ROLES WITHIN THE GOVERNMENT

Prime Minister – accepts responsibility when everything is going well and blames his minions when everything is going badly.

Chancellor of the Exchequer – makes hugely successful decisions on money matters, which the Prime Minister then takes credit for.

The Cabinet – named after the storage unit that the Prime Minister uses to keep them in.

The Opposition – not to be confused with the **Civil Service**. Their job is to obstruct the decisions of the Prime Minister and win high approval ratings by being a pain in the arse.

Backbenchers – their job is to waste time by asking the Prime Minister questions about the shortage of parking spaces in their constituency.

The Speaker – their job is to say 'Order' during Parliament meetings, and to keep their spouses out of trouble.

Number 10

The Prime Minister of the United Kingdom famously lives at **Number 10 Downing Street** in London, although technically they should live at Number 11, as 10 is not a prime number.

The most famous part of the house is the black front door. The hinges on the door are faulty, so a police officer is employed to prop it up 24/7. It's also his duty to keep ex-Prime Minister Gordon Brown from returning and squatting.

THE BUDGET

The **Budget** is annually delivered live on TV by the Chancellor of the Exchequer, and is often mistaken for *The Muppet Show*. It is a summary of how much money the UK public needs to give to the Government to increase economic growth and to finance the MPs' Christmas lunch.

The speech (economics homework) is carried to Parliament in the Chancellor's red budget box (lunchbox) and has normally been dreamt up the night before.

One has suggested that for the foreseeable future he delivers his speech whilst wearing a balaclava. Even highwayman Dick Turpin had the decency to cover his face before robbing people.

Yes, in life there will always be death and taxes. However, death doesn't get worse every year. The key points of the Budget are normally summarised on *Crimewatch*.

The Government has a two-pronged crisis-resolution programme, which can be implemented should everything go wrong, with the aim of encouraging economic recovery. The programme is:

1   Offer the economy a generous loan from Wonga.

2   Mass governmental suicide.

POLITICAL PARTIES OF THE UNITED KINGDOM

LABOUR PARTY

The **Labour Party** was formed to give a voice to the many millions of people belonging to the Working Class – a task normally attempted in recent years by someone who's privately educated or has millions in the bank, or both.

CONSERVATIVE PARTY

The **Conservative Party** is run by toffs who work exclusively in the interests of the super-rich. This party works hard to give as much money to bankers as possible, and sign away as much British democracy as possible to the European Union. Voting for a complete Tory government would be a guaranteed way of getting *Spitting Image* back on television.

LIBERAL DEMOCRAT PARTY

The **Liberal Democrats (Lib Dems/Fib Dems)** are generally considered to be a wasted vote having recently achieved promotion from the wastepaper bin to 'None of the above' on UK electoral voting slips. One is fairly sure the party is dominated by male members due to the difficulty of applying make-up onto two faces.

BRITISH NATIONAL PARTY

The **British National Party (BNP)** is fully committed to the defence of British genes and purity despite not being born with any DNA themselves. It is their sole purpose in life to argue that 'Immigration is so high within the British Isles that only 200 more immigrants are required to completely sink it.'

UK INDEPENDENCE PARTY

The **UK Independence Party (UKIP)** is the political party for people who find the BNP a little too scary and prefer their racism disguised.

CURRENT GOVERNMENT AND POLITICIANS OF THE UNITED KINGDOM

The voters of the general election in 2010 were undecided, resulting in a Government that was well and truly hung.

DAVID 'CALL ME DAVE' CAMERON

David Cameron is the current Prime Minister of the United Kingdom, although one seriously doubts whether he passed his A-level Politics at all. He consistently concludes that the economy is in a terrible mess due to ~~the banking collapse~~ Labour. If one had a pound for every time Cameron said he would sort out the country's problems, one would be rich enough to live under a Tory government. The land of dope and Tory ...

NICK CLEGG

Being the Deputy Prime Minister means **Nick Clegg** gets full control of important Government matters, such as sitting next to Mr Cameron in the Commons and looking after his office when he's somewhere more important. He failed his A-level Biology after he couldn't find a backbone. There are two things generally considered unlikeable about Mr Clegg. His face.

GEORGE OSBORNE

The Chancellor of the Exchequer. **George Osborne** is one of the wealthiest members of the Cabinet, who was born with a silver spoon in his mouth, which he subsequently swallowed. He gained a respectable 9 A*–C GCSE grades, but one believes he cannot have done any better than scraping an F in economics, as he has tremendous difficulty with his multiplication. Thank God for that – one Osborne is bad enough. He has blamed everything, including the weather, for the shrinking economy; next on his list are sunshine, moonlight, good times and the boogie. Despite the clear need for drastic action, Mr Osborne maintains that the UK economic recovery is 'on track'. One assumes it's soundly tied down, and the train is due any minute.

THERESA MAY

The Home Secretary has the power to refuse entry to the UK to anyone deemed unfavourable to the public good, which is precisely why **Theresa May** has a photograph of Piers Morgan in her purse. He's America's problem now.

ED MILIBAND

Ed Miliband is the leader of the Labour Party and star of British sitcom, *Mr Bean*. One is desperately looking for more useful information on this man. Watch this space.

NIGEL FARAGE

Nigel Farage is the leader of the UK Independence Party. He wants to get rid of immigrants working within the UK whilst employing his German wife as a secretary.

BORIS JOHNSON

The Mayor of London, the British seemingly love **Mr Johnson** for his charismatic charm, nutty-professor hair and his proven track record of putting his foot (or his pen) in his mouth. He has been described as a 'bumbling buffoon' but being educated at Eton College means he's much cleverer than he looks, and sounds. He doesn't really understand anything about politics or London, but won his mayoral election for having the tidiest desk. Boris is also a talented footballer, appearing in a charity match and successfully tackling a German, something that Steven Gerrard has failed to do since 2001.

LARRY THE CAT
Larry the Cat is the Chief Mouser to the Cabinet Office. Known to have caught other various vermin including Michael Gove, Ed Balls and Jeremy Hunt.

EX-PRIME MINISTERS
WINSTON CHURCHILL (B. 1874 D. 1965)
Winston Churchill was the first Prime Minister to give the Germans a very British two-fingered salute during the Second World War and has become the standard by which other Prime Ministers are measured. Turning adversity to strength, his many speeches are remembered to this day. In 1940 he told apprehensive Britons:

> We shall fight on the beaches, we shall fight on the landing grounds, we shall fight in the fields, during football matches, we shall fight in the hills, beside swimming pools and on

street corners outside the pubs after closing
time; we shall never surrender.

Every word in that speech is part of the
English language, except one. *'Surrender'* is of
course French.

Neville Chamberlain's 'This has all gone tits
up' speech the previous year might not have
had the same rallying effect.

Churchill spoke fluent Italian, which he used to
full effect by making prank calls to Adolf Hitler
claiming he was Benito Mussolini and encouraging the German leader to invade Russia.
When the USA was attacked by Japan in
December 1941, Churchill organised a party at
Buckingham Palace where important American
military leaders were drunk under the table
and persuaded to defeat Germany first before
Japan. Churchill said this was his 'proudest
achievement' – even if it meant remortgaging
the British Empire to help pay the bar bill.

MARGARET THATCHER (B. 1925 D. 2013)
Margaret Thatcher was the longest-serving, most beloved/hated Prime Minister in British history. Things were so bad in 1979 that the British Government was willing to put their trust in a woman, who it turned out was medically proven to have larger balls than any other post-war Prime Minister.

Margaret Thatcher was often compared to Florence Nightingale – the lady with the lamp. Unfortunately Thatcher's lamp turned out to be a blowlamp.

During her time in power, she kept money flowing into the UK by selling anything that moved. To her, nothing was off-limits. She sold power companies, communication networks, her husband's false teeth and children's souls. Her tireless campaigning against political trends, social classes and racial groups of

society has since been taken over by the
Daily Mail.

Amongst her great and glorious accomplish-
ments were the re-establishment of the British
Empire and bringing some much-needed
housekeeping tips to Number 10.

In 1982, Argentine fascists invaded the
Falklands, a small bunch of islands no one had
even heard of until that year. Alarmed at the
economic impact of falling Union Flag sales,
Mrs Thatcher had no option but to wipe out
the natives that lived there in an attempt to
get a 100 per cent vote of confidence for her
actions by the remaining Islanders. The
Falklands belonged to Great Britain anyway,
so it wasn't a war, more of a homecoming.
One doesn't care if it would make consider-
ably more geographical sense for them to
belong to Argentina. They're ours, because
one says so.

Margaret Thatcher's funeral.
Over-eighteens only. No miners.

Mrs Thatcher died in April 2013. Considering the damage she did to the British steel industry, one is surprised she managed to find a bucket to kick. Arrangements for her state funeral were quickly put into practice, although surely it should've been privatised? Members of Parliament put a fair bit of consideration into renaming the August bank holiday in her honour. One can't think of a more fitting tribute to her defining legacy than telling people not to bother going to work on the Monday.

JOHN MAJOR (B. 1943)

John Major is often regarded as one of the greatest Prime Ministers, although only by himself. Under his rule, Great Britain became 'the grey island' in acknowledgement of the fact that it now had the most boring leader in its considerable history.

Following his celebrated leaving of Parliament, it was revealed that he had had an affair with Conservative Party colleague Edwina Currie. His wife hadn't suspected anything, though one would have thought Mr Major's cheerful catchphrase 'Just popping out for some hot curry' would have been a dead giveaway.

TONY BLAIR (B. 1953)

Tony Blair served as the Prime Minister of the United Kingdom, the fifty-first state of the United States of America, from 1997 to 2007.

Every year, tax money equating to £2 million would be used to protect Mr Blair. He employed people specifically to stand beside him, intimidate anyone who approached and generally look frightening. This caused a considerable amount of confusion within the Royal Family, as we all assumed that was Cherie Blair's job. She would often compare her husband to Churchill, which seems funny, as she looks more like a bulldog than he does.

Mr Blair admitted he was once a borderline alcoholic. Just imagine the amount of panic, waking up the next morning with a hangover, realising you've invaded Iraq.

Despite everyone being vaccinated against TB, Tony Blair managed to keep coming back by winning three elections in a row, a record for the Labour Party. This gave him the perfect excuse to flash his horrible smile all the bloody time, something that an Act of Parliament now prevents him from doing within the UK's borders.

Tony Blair divides his retirement between England and the Middle East, where he is still currently searching for weapons of mass destruction. His autobiography can be bought at any Waterstones bookshop, often located in the 'Fiction' or 'Crime' sections.

CHAPTER 4

Culture

One might be biased, but no one else on the planet comes close to our great genius.

LANGUAGE

The English language is spoken by an estimated 95 per cent of the British population. It is the first language of 400 billion people globally and the second language of 400 billion more. Being the most widely spoken language on Earth, it is the closest thing we have to a global common tongue. It began with the phrase 'Up yours, Caesar' as the Roman emperor vacated Great Britain, after deciding there was no place like Rome. He came, he saw, he left.

The **Queen's English** is the one truly correct version of English, spoken only by Her Majesty and some of her friends, the Royal Family, the BBC – before standards slipped – and

anyone who is not a moron doomed to fail
in life.

British accents are charming and singsongy
– the dullest story sounds interesting and the
thickest person sounds brilliant. On behalf of
the British public, one would like to apologise
to the American people if our accent makes us
sound superior. It's because we are. If the
American nation had a British accent, they'd
never shut up.

Most of the British population doesn't have an
accent. It's just how things should sound when
pronounced properly.

It is often said that but for the bravery of our
soldiers during the Second World War we
would all be speaking German by now. This is
simply rubbish, as the British people are
pretty bloody awful at learning other
languages. Even the soldiers of Germany and
Japan spoke fluent English, as depicted in most

war films. It is a well-known fact that the English language has the miraculous ability to translate itself into words immediately understood by any foreign subject when spoken very loudly.

LITERATURE

Great Britain has a great reputation as a nation full of literary geniuses. You can walk into any public house throughout the country and almost guarantee it will be full of writers and poets. In most other countries they're called drunks.

CHARLES DICKENS

Charles Dickens was an English writer, generally regarded as the greatest novelist of the Victorian period, whose stories include *Oliver Twist* and *The Muppet Christmas Carol*. He became much admired for his portrayals of life amongst the lower orders of society. 'It was the best of times, it was the worst of times', but then he had never lived under a Labour government.

Robert Burns

To the Scottish, **Robert Burns** is every bit as important as William Shakespeare. The poet wrote in English and in Scots dialect, just to confuse everyone. He is probably best known for writing the poem 'Auld Lang Syne'. The title roughly translates to 'The good old days', which he meant sarcastically, of course, as nothing good has ever happened in Scotland.

Customarily, the singing of 'Auld Lang Syne' and alcohol are inseparable, thus making the song tolerable. The tradition of crossing arms whilst singing this song was started by the Scots, mainly in a bid to protect their wallets.

Jane Austen

Jane Austen is one of the most widely read writers in English literature. She practically created the genre of romantic fiction and is solely responsible for the brooding manliness of Colin Firth, the housewife's favourite. She has written TV shows, films, books and ebooks, including *Pride and Prejudice,* the story of Elizabeth Bennet and Mr Darcy that the BBC remakes three sodding times a year. The recent republished zombie version has pretty much the same premise, except with more swordfights and zombies, roughly making it 500 per cent more bearable. Austen's books have had at least 214 film or TV adaptations, none of which any male has watched voluntarily.

BRONTË SISTERS

Charlotte is mostly famous for her eponymous novel, *Jane Eyre,* an epic tale of love, coming of age and crazy women locked up in attics.

Emily was of a much darker temperament than her older sister. Spending most of her time in the native towns of Yorkshire gave her inspiration to write *Wuthering Heights*, an epic tale of hardly hidden inbreeding in rural England.

It is believed that the youngest sister, **Anne**, didn't really do much of anything.

THEATRE

British theatre is a two-and a-half-hour, live-action, barely affordable, un-lip-synced version of *Glee*.

Avid followers of musical theatre have been led into the light by **Andrew Lloyd Webber**, who has changed the face of London's **West End**; one just wishes the West End would return the favour.

If you are thinking of visiting the theatre, then one of the main things you need to consider is which seats you are going to buy: the stalls (ground floor), the dress or royal circle (first floor) or the upper circle (third floor). There are also the royal boxes (second floor, at a right angle to the stage and the rest of the audience). These will only ever be occupied by people who want to be seen, and not see. One can confirm the views are absolutely atrocious.

Royal Attendance

Members of the Royal Family that attend social engagements such as the Royal Variety Performance are there for one of three reasons:

1 They've drawn the short straw. Unlucky.

2 The ticket had no buyers on eBay.

3 There's sod all to watch on television.

Phantom of the Opera

Phantom of the Opera is generally considered
to be one of Andrew Lloyd Webber's greatest
works due to its clichés, reprises, annoying
characters that spend most of their stage
time crying and yet more reprises. The stage
production has been exported to other cities,
including New York, where it is currently the
longest-running show on Broadway. Eighteen
years after opening, *Phantom of the Opera*
was finally adapted for the big screen by the
overly flamboyant film director, Joel
Schumacher, the same person who put
nipples on Batman's suit. Lord Webber
wasn't particularly happy with the result, as
the onscreen film characters weren't half as
annoying as he originally intended them to
be.

Mamma Mia!

Mamma Mia! is a musical based on the works
of Swedish pop group ABBA. The film adaption

starred Meryl Streep and Pierce Brosnan, whose singing voices are sometimes used by the Metropolitan Police as a weapon to help disperse rioters. The main story is based around one woman trying to discover which one of her three ex-lovers is the biological father of her teenage daughter. One thinks it should've been called *Jeremy Kyle – The Musical* instead.

WILLIAM SHAKESPEARE

William Shakespeare was born in Stratford-upon-Avon and is the most celebrated English playwright and poet. He has been bullying teachers and students since 1564.

His most famous publication is *The Complete Works of William Shakespeare*. The comedies, tragedies, histories and sonnets contained within add up to hours of bewilderment, boredom and disrespect when taught in class. His *Complete Shopping Lists*, however, are regarded as some of the greatest works of

English literature and have provided scholars with endless debate and discussion.

A theory of probability suggests that with enough time, a collection of monkeys with typewriters could reproduce the works of Shakespeare. It took four monkeys thirty minutes to write *Fifty Shades of Grey* and thirty seconds to write the autobiography of Jedward.

In his later years, Shakespeare stopped writing plays and concentrated on poetry instead, which effectively meant he was going from bard to verse.

If William Shakespeare were alive today, he'd most certainly be writing a comedy/tragedy sitcom on the calamities of the Coalition Government.

Common Phrases

Shakespeare invented more words than most people even know and is responsible for some common phrases that we still use today:

- Knock, knock. Who's there?

- Good riddance.

- Laughing stock.

- For goodness sake.

- Dead as a doornail.

- You dipstick, Rodney.

- I'm lovin' it.

- Morning benders.

- Yeah, boy!

PANTOMIME

Pantomime is a great and unique British tradition and something, amongst other things, that's impossible to explain to an American. It is a participatory form of theatre, in which members of the audience are expected to sing along and shout out phrases to the performers on stage. (Oh no they aren't!)

When actors are too old, lazy or dull to appear in anything else, they can spend their lonely Christmas on stage with other minor celebrities. A glittering TV and showbiz career? It's behind you!

Theatre Etiquette

This is most important. In order to make everyone's experience enjoyable, here are some basic suggestions as to what is acceptable:

- As soon as the theatre goes dark, it is a good idea to shut up. Talking or (God forbid) failing to turn off your mobile phone will earn you a death stare, or worse. Contrary to popular belief, falling asleep is acceptable, as one did during *Les Misérables*. This was of course due to French history being utterly sodding tedious. One certainly came out more *misérable*. Camilla said, 'I've never seen so much shit; and I've got a stable full of horses.'

- Everyone coughs from time to time, but if you're about to expire from a coughing fit, it seems only fair, for those around you and the person who'd have to clean up your body, that you step outside.

- Refrain from taking photographs during the performance. Everyone knows actors are shy.

- During the interval, try not to get too drunk, or the second act may prove challenging.

- Only heckle if you're absolutely positive you've come to see a pantomime.

- Always stand to let other theatregoers pass by you, unless they're French tourists, in which case tripping them is encouraged.

- People getting busy with each other in the back row is like a traffic accident; you don't want to look, but you can't look away. Voyeurism isn't British; it's pornography. And disgusting.

- When the show has come to a complete stop, you are fully expected to clap once, and then clap again. Stopping this noisy show of appreciation before the actors'

10 millionth encore is fine, but only if you're prepared to back up your snub with a critical comment on the performance, like when Mother described the rumbling sound effects within *We Will Rock You* as Freddie Mercury turning in his grave at the public butchering of his beloved songs.

• A standing ovation is a genuine rarity, but the ultimate seal of approval. This shows your appreciation of the talent you have just witnessed on stage and gives you the chance to stretch your legs after spending three hours sitting in a chair designed for an infant.

MUSIC

This relatively small island has made a huge impact on the music industry, producing some of the most memorable performers and groups of all time. And Cheryl Cole. Whilst television first brought us the everyday sights of British life, British music has provided the soundtrack to our lives.

BRITISH INVASION

The **British Invasion** was a phenomenon that occurred during the swinging sixties when rock and pop music acts invaded the United States of America for the first time since 1812.

Encouraged by his love of fancy dress, Prince Harry went to a swinging sixties house party dressed as a hippy, totally unaware it would be full of sixty-year-old swingers. Awkward.

THE FAB FOUR

The **Beatles** are Great Britain's finest export since civilisation, HP Sauce, PG Tips and the Aston Martin, and are by far the undisputed champions of British music.

The mop-topped foursome still remain the most influential band from the sixties and are credited with introducing more pop-music innovations than any other group in the world. Hysterical fans screamed, with some even fainting, mainly from the shock of seeing four young lads from Liverpool with actual paid jobs.

Despite their best efforts to make everyone love each other, the affection within the band dimmed and Beatlemania officially ended in 1970. It seems money really can't buy you love.

THE STONES

The **Rolling Stones** are the longest-surviving British rock band. Despite collecting their bus passes and weekly pension, they still believe the year is 1963 and simply refuse to disappear.

Lead singer Mick Jagger is famously known for his dancing skills, which are a cross between a person with a nervous disposition and someone who has messed themselves.

The Stones came out of retirement for a final farewell tour seven tours ago. Don't despair if you failed to buy tickets. The event can be recreated simply by visiting your local old people's home on karaoke night.

QUEEN

One of the top three greatest bands to ever come out of London, **Queen** had a phenomenal impact on the worldwide music scene. Formed in 1970 by friends Freddie Mercury, Brian May, Roger Taylor and some guy who played bass guitar as an alternative option to manual labour.

Freddie Mercury was known for his flamboyant stage presence, but was also laid-back and shy when out of the spotlight. He never elaborated much on his sexuality. And judging by the costumes he wore, he didn't really have to.

The X Factor

The X Factor is a British television music competition that gives talentless wannabes the chance to humiliate themselves, their families and their towns in front of an audience of millions. Recent celebrity judges have been the 'absolutely fantastic' Gary Barlow and the 'hard to understand' Cheryl Cole.

Essentially *The X Factor* is an ingenious four-month advertising campaign disguised as a TV talent competition. It could possibly be the only TV show where the adverts can't come quick enough.

ONE DIRECTION

One Direction are an English pop band consisting of five little boys who have achieved worldwide success despite the fact none of them can sing.

The manufactured defective band became successful in 2010, after which Simon Cowell decided to further exploit musically illiterate teenage girls with songs about: going out with girls, talking about how beautiful girls are, and so on.

The One Direction film *This Is Us* has so far grossed over 4 million in the UK. You can add another person to the list, after it made one feel nauseous for the full ninety minutes.

Be assured. One Direction are not and never will be bigger or better than The Beatles. If it remotely looks like they're achieving such status, one will have them temporarily locked inside Wandsworth Prison until things start to calm down again. Yes, they are catchy, but so was the plague.

GARY BARLOW

Gary Barlow has sold over 50 million records worldwide, raised millions for charity, was an instrumental cog in the success of Mother's Diamond Jubilee celebrations and has avoided paying £20 million in tax to the Treasury. Investigations revealed that Gary Barlow wrote 4 million love songs, but only declared 1 million for tax reasons. One can confirm that Gary Barlow has been degraded from OBE to IOU. All this time one thought he played the piano, turns out he's on the fiddle.

Although, one can't help feeling slightly sorry for the poor man. Whatever he said, whatever he did, he didn't mean it.

SIR CLIFF RICHARD

Sir Cliff Richard is so awe-inspiringly awful you can only love him. He is a very private man who refuses to discuss anything about his personal life. One wishes he would just come out and admit what we've all suspected for years; his songs are terrible.

COLDPLAY

The British public has become increasingly divided over the musical 'talent' of **Coldplay**. Half the nation thinks they're the biggest bunch of untalented dribble ever created and the other half have never actually listened to them.

EUROVISION

Eurovision is an annual karaoke competition featuring the largest gathering of fake-tanned Europeans outside Essex. We may not win the prestigious prize very often, but at least the UK will always beat America.

 Text from the Greek President: '8 points to the country to the left, 10 to the right and 12 to the country that bail us out.'

The UK was represented by Bonnie Tyler in the 2013 contest. Her chances of winning were ranked at 50–1, which was more than generous to say the least. Quite frankly, after hearing the song one was holding out for a zero. Once upon a time we were ruling the world, now we're only falling apart.

One is becoming sick of the political and tactical voting – the tactics in question being 'don't vote for the UK, because their song was rubbish' or 'vote for the country that you don't want invading you'. Europe likes the UK enough to sing their songs in our language, but not enough to give us some sodding points.

One is seriously considering holding a referendum on getting the UK out of Eurovision.

FILM
The British film industry is one of the most successful film industries in the world, where smuggling sweets into the cinema has almost become as British as a cup of tea. Its wise and far-sighted producers are afraid of any form of innovation and originality and endlessly remake

the same types of films, including: posh dramas, romantic comedies with Hugh Grant, working-class comedies, big-screen outings and the horrendous films of Danny Dyer.

007

James Bond is a top-secret spy and star of a long-running film franchise, although he would be much better at his official role if he didn't keep telling everyone who he was. You can contact Bond by simply phoning 007, or +44 07 when outside the UK.

Over the years, Agent 007 has made a huge impact on the culture of the world, with people introducing themselves with their surnames first, everyone wanting an Aston Martin and Mike Myers remaining relevant for far longer than he should have.

The Bond films are an instant favourite on television for one and the family over Christmas. The humour is as dry as a properly shaken not stirred Martini and their simple plots mean that even the most intoxicated, unconscious member of the family can follow the storyline.

One has had an interesting time meeting with Sean Connery, Roger Moore, Timothy Dalton, Pierce Brosnan and Daniel Craig over the years, but not so much with George Lazenby; one doesn't think we had enough time to bond. Not entirely sure Daniel Craig was impressed with Camilla's idea of becoming the next Bond girl.

CARRY ON

The **Carry On** franchise was a series of low-budget comedic films, characterised by slapstick, double entendres, farce and sexual innuendo. There is no truth to the rumour that these classic films were loosely based on the testaments of Operation Yewtree.

*

The greatest unanswered question in life still remains: 'At a British cinema, which armrest is yours?'

Harry Potter

The wizarding world of **Harry Potter** is one of the highest-grossing franchises of all time and has seen a huge cast list come and go throughout the ten years it took to make the eight films. Daniel Radcliffe revealed that he was dependent on alcohol to make it through the final films. That makes two of us.

TELEVISION

The world's first television was invented by **John Logie Baird**, a Scottish man who was too tight to spend his evenings down the pub.

Television in Britain got its big break in June 1953, when approximately 20 million viewers crowded around to watch Queen Elizabeth II's coronation. For years to come it would be Mother's annual duty to give a short reflective speech to the nation on Christmas Day, or as she calls it, *The One Show*.

BBC

Depending on your opinion, the **British Broadcasting Corporation (BBC)** is either a wonderful British institution that is worth its weight in gold or a money pit propaganda merchant for Britain's Left Wing. The BBC has been responsible for all of Britain's most-loved radio and television programmes, including *Sherlock*, *Newsnight* and *Flog It!*

Doctor Who

Great Britain has given the world many questionable things over the years, including kidney pie, queueing and H from Steps. But, one television show makes up for all of that. *Doctor*

Who is the longest-running science-fiction show in history, albeit with a short 16-year break when someone accidentally closed the Tardis door with the keys still inside.

Doctor Who's main archenemies are the Daleks, whose famous catchphrase 'Abdicate' has become culturally renowned throughout Britain. At least one thinks that's what they're saying.

One has had the pleasure of visiting the set of the new *Doctor Who* in Wales. The NHS cutbacks are so severe that his main office is inside a phone box. Poor sod.

Soap Operas

EastEnders and *Coronation Street* are British television soap operas, particularly popular with the older generation, the unemployed, schoolchildren, retirement homes and the chronically depressed. Viewers of these programmes may have a variety of other conditions including grottiness, lazyarthritis or being utterly devoid of culture.

Cast members provide the vast majority of Britain with a fly-on-the-wall look at life, where simple pleasures – such as adultery, murder, abduction and having a drink in the local public house, where the pints flow and the plot thickens – keep the mostly working-class community happy.

British soaps are generally supposed to be true to life, though one thinks they're about as realistic as seeing a corgi filling in tax papers whilst whistling Stravinsky's *The Rite of Spring* in A-minor.

I'm a Celebrity ... Get Me Out of Here!
This is a British television show in which twelve ageing and desperate Z-list celebrities are locked inside a large greenhouse within the convict-infested jungle of Australia.

In order to qualify to appear on the show, celebrities must be completely washed up and incapable of being any use to society whatsoever. Luckily, Britain is full of such people. Celebrities who appear on the show are paid a fee to compensate for any lack of earnings they may experience. In reality, the fee corresponds to the level of unemployment benefits they have lost.

During the series, contestants must complete daily tasks to earn rations of celery, rice and testicles most likely belonging to Skippy the Bush Kangaroo.

If anymore Z-list celebrities end up helping Scotland Yard with their enquiries, one will consider setting the next series inside a prison.

PERIOD DRAMAS

Period dramas are invariably an adaptation of a book or play written at least 100 years ago, often described as 'Carry On films without the jokes'.

Downton Abbey is the turn-of-the-century British period drama about etiquette and social scandal. It is like *Big Brother* to the Royal Family. This television show has become a cultural phenomenon, being a major success on both sides of the Atlantic. Yet everything about that success seems illogical; the plot is painfully slow, the dialogue is unnecessarily dry and one really cannot understand how Downton Abbey runs with so few staff.

QUIZ SHOWS

The *Weakest Link* is a British television game show in which MPs must answer general-knowledge questions to create a chain of money. This money (annual budget) must be banked for it to be part of the final prize at the end of the show. After each round, the MPs must vote off one of their own. The final two contestants enter a head-to-head debate, where the winner is sworn into Government as the newly elected Prime Minister.

The British game show *Countdown* was invented in Wales, however, it was quickly dropped when they ran out of consonants. The first time one watched it, one got aroused, but then that's only seven letters.

Visual Arts

When it comes to art appreciation, the British tend to be very nervous. If the painting tells a story, so much the better. If they can't understand what it's trying to depict, they tend to close their eyes and stick their fingers in their ears.

It is a little known fact that modern artists always sign their names at the bottom of their paintings so that people will know which way to hang them.

NATIONAL GALLERY

The **National Gallery** in London houses one of the finest collections of Western European paintings in the world from 1250 onwards. Its masterpieces include artworks from Michelangelo, Rembrandt and Year 3 of Rooks Nest Primary School, as well as the private collections of Tony Hart and Neil Buchanan.

Banksy

Banksy is the anonymous British graffiti artist from Bristol, who uses public walls as a canvas and is currently the most wanted person under the Anti-social Behaviour Act 2003.

TRACEY EMIN

Tracey Emin is a supposed artist, whose conceptual artwork, which basically means she can't draw or paint, is the remnants of a bizarre and perverse life.

Her most famous piece of 'art' was a tent appliquéd with the names of everyone she had ever slept with. She has since been commissioned to create a marquee for Katie Price.

ANGEL OF THE NORTH

Whilst approaching Gateshead on the M1, you will be greeted by what looks like a rusty, metal crucifix. The notorious, creaking sculpture, the *Angel of the North*, known locally as the *Gateshead Flasher*, has been voted 'the second worst thing in Britain every year since its completion in 1998. It is pipped to the title annually by Russell Brand.

ARCHITECTURE

Every country in the world shares the same basic building blocks: brick, stone, steel, mortar and McDonald's restaurants. But architecture is what sets them apart.

STONEHENGE

Stonehenge is a must-see ancient monument

for any tourist visiting the British Isles. There is much speculation by historians as to why it was built: the country's first football stadium, a religious site, a prison far too easy to escape or an astronomical observatory to establish calendar date, time and season. The timing would've been right when it was first built, but they failed to think about the clocks going forward.

Stonehenge has an unfinished look about it, probably as it went over budget. One thing you will notice whilst visiting is the remarkable condition that the souvenir shop is in – despite its age. Archaeologists believe Stonehenge was built anywhere from 3000 BC to 2000 BC, but the exact date is unknown as they are unable to read the small-print details on the original planning permission sent to Wiltshire Council. How they managed to get planning permission for green-belt land in the first place is just another one of its ancient mysteries.

ST PAUL'S CATHEDRAL

One of the most recognisable symbols of London since the completion of its current domed incarnation in 1711, **St Paul's Cathedral** has managed to appear in everything from *Mary Poppins* to *Doctor Who*. Not bad for a building that nearly didn't make it through the Second World War.

In 1940, Germany was playing a game of 'Let's see how many bombs we can drop on London', with a huge domed building being too obvious to miss. Thankfully the Germans aren't as good at hitting the bombing target as they are at taking penalties. Divine intervention had occurred and faith in God had been restored.

MILLENNIUM DOME

The **Millennium Dome** was an overgrown tent in London, thrown together as a doomed cultural landmark to celebrate the new millennium.

When originally opened, it featured ambitious exhibitions inside. But, being organised by the Government, it turned out to be rubbish, so it was closed within the year. The Conservative Party has rubbed this in Labour's face ever since.

For many years after it was used as a rather convenient shelter for the public against the British weather, until it was re-christened in 2005 as the O2. It now serves as a daycare centre for musicians such as Lady Gaga and Justin Bieber when they are begrudgingly allowed into the country.

LONDON EYE

One could say seeing London is easy on the **London Eye**, originating from a failed, insane Boris Johnson project to build the world's biggest bicycle. Its other name is the Millennium Wheel, but nobody calls it that. Ever. The Eye offers a unique, 360-degree, pigeon-eye view of London and the sludgy contents of the River Thames.

During London Fashion Week officials decided to cover the Eye in camouflage, although one really couldn't see the attraction.

FOLKLORE
ROBIN HOOD

Kevin Costner, who later renamed himself **Robin Hood** to avoid deportation, is a legendary figure from English folklore whose tales make up the entirety of what Americans know about medieval times. Often portrayed as handsome and charming, the legend of this fox of a man has lasted since the early thirteenth century, when Nottingham was full of drunks, easy women and thieving teenagers. Not a lot has changed since.

Robin Hood is not a lone outlaw, but the leader of a trained band of fighters. He is said to have hung around with a band of 'merry men', though it is uncertain whether this meant they were a cheery bunch or the usual British drunkards, who spent their days 'stealing from the rich and giving to the poor'. This philosophy has since been adopted by the British Government, albeit, vice versa.

Robin Hood was victorious, but as he owed money in taxes he temporarily moved to Spain to avoid the authorities.

In 1247, Robin Hood lay dying and all the faithful gathered round. With his weak and fading breath, Robin asked Maid Marian to bring him the best arrow and then asked Little John to bring him his bow. He put the arrow to the bow and aimed through the open window into the generous green of Sherwood Forest beyond that he loved so much. He asked of Friar Tuck, 'Promise me that wherever the arrow falls, there you will bury me.' And when the friar had sworn, with his last strength he pulled on the bow and let the arrow fly. And then Robin Hood died, smiling.

The next day, they did exactly as promised and buried him on top of his wardrobe.

Loch Ness Monster

The **Loch Ness Monster** is a large creature that inhabits Loch Ness in the Scottish Highlands. It is an extremely shy beast that only reveals itself to those with little or no means of capturing solid evidence of its existence. It is estimated that the monster's annual contribution to the Scottish economy is equivalent to the sale of 40 million tartan tea towels from Aberdeen market.

FOOD

'Food, glorious, food. Roast swan and mustard.'

Generally, when one hears the phrase 'British cuisine' spoken beyond the British Isles, it is safely assumed to be the punchline to a joke.

Having the Middletons over for dinner tonight. Camilla's just showing them how to hold a knife and fork properly.

Carole Middleton uses a revolutionary method of creating home cuisine, which has never been seen within the realms of modern royalty. It is known as the ping technique, or more commonly as the microwave oven. One has seen more appetising things come out the back of a corgi.

In the UK the word 'deep-fried' is seen more as a term of culinary reassurance than as a threat to health. Anything deep-fried and containing trace amounts of nutrients is generally considered luxurious. People who don't like deep-fried food in Britain are viewed with great suspicion.

Deep-fried Mars bar (aka The Last Supper) is a health-food product invented by the Scottish. After eating a deep-fried Mars bar, the consumer will generally enter a state of sugar-induced coma, potentially followed by death.

It is worth remembering that there is no British food that cannot be improved immeasurably by the addition of the very lifeblood of Britain: **gravy**.

Australia may be the undisputed kings of the barbecue, but it's the Brits who show the most dedication. At the first glimpse of sunshine British men will dust off the grill, wear their comedy aprons and doggedly toss the burgers throughout the guaranteed downpour until burnt on the outside and raw on the inside.

Of course, it goes without saying that all British-made food can be washed down your throat nicely with a titanic-sized **gin**. Easy on the ice.

TOP BRITISH FOODS

It's little wonder that British cuisine is so often considered a joke. One finds the names given to some of our dishes really quite laughable.

CRUMPET

A **thick, flat, savoury cake** with a soft texture, made from a yeast mixture cooked on a griddle and eaten toasted and buttered. British man cannot live on bread alone; he needs a little crumpet too.

BACON SANDWICH

The year was 1762. The date was 19 November. As the peasants living in Sandwich, England, awoke, each one found there to be a distinct smell in the air. Sadly, the smell turned out to be the sudden, unexpected release of a large underground supply of methane gas. But, it was this day in 1762 that the 4th Earl of Sandwich became the single most important man in British history by ordering **succulent rashers of bacon between two slices of bread**.

SUNDAY ROAST

The ultimate expression of Britishness – society simply cannot operate without a weekly helping of succulent **meat and two veg**. Any British person who does not crave this meal with all the trimmings is practically guilty of treason.

HAGGIS

A Scottish delicacy, which contrary to popular belief is not a mythical creature, roaming free on the hillside. It is a **savoury pudding made from sheep's offal**, which is supposed to have been eaten as far back as the ninth century, but has no known place of origin; most likely because nobody ever wanted to admit it was their idea.

DONER KEBAB

This involves **unidentified slices of meat, stuffed inside a pitta bread.** Carved from a spit-roasted God-knows-what, holding a kebab means you have finally exhausted your powers of reason and common sense. The only chance of survival is to make sure you've had a full dosage of medicine (alcohol) before consumption.

TV Chefs

The world of cookery programmes in Britain has moved on since the days of dear old **Fanny Cradock**. Britain currently has more TV chefs than one's had hot dinners.

Delia Smith is an English cook and television presenter, both whilst playing football, whose main courses are big enough for a family of four, provided the family is not very hungry.

Nigella Lawson is the most luscious-lipped British chef on television, where she serves enough bowls of sexual innuendo to make Mrs Beeton blush. Without her, men and women would never have imagined licking their fingers and caressing a ladle whilst cooking in their underwear.

Jamie Oliver, the tongue-in-cheeky-chappie, took this new culinary approach to the extreme and started cooking under the nickname 'The Naked Chef'. He single-handedly cooks every school dinner in England every day.

Gordon Ramsay is known for his love of food, a three-Michelin-star ready-meals restaurant in London and very occasional swearing.

DRINK

Drinking is an enormous part of British heritage and culture. It's a toss-up whether the British love their tea or their alcohol more. Whether it's beer-fuelled football hooligans, gin-soaked royals or whisky-doused politicians, getting plastered is a national pastime.

Most Brits never refuse a drink, with a few stiff ones required for important business decisions, establishing a relationship or buying furniture. The Yeoman of the Drinks Cabinet is on hand twenty-four hours a day, seven days a week for thirsty royals, with the Secondary Minister on standby in case of fume intoxication.

BRITISH BEER/LAGER

This is absolutely 100 per cent the best drink in the world, if you like the taste of your cat's piss. Principally consumed by louts who believe they have a sense of humour, **beer** is the most common cause of drunk driving owing to the fact it is often drunk by the gallon.

REAL ALE

A more traditional drink, being the favourite tipple of Princess Anne and every working man. **Real ale** forms part of social traditions such as beer festivals, pub-crawling and fighting.

CIDER

Cider is an alcoholic liquid made mostly from apples. Back in the day it was only drunk by farmers and schoolchildren standing on street corners, but recently cider has refermented itself higher up the class ladder. Compared to most parts of the country, where it is still used as a specialist form of nail-polish remover, the real potent stuff comes from the West Country, where everyone talks, drinks and sings like The Wurzels.

WINE

Wine varies in quality. Any bottle of wine under £5 will resemble a mixture of diluted fruit juice and paint thinner.

ALCOPOPS

Very much a part of the British way of life during the youth alcohol crisis of the 1990s, **alcopops** have contributed immensely to the rising population. They are very popular amongst feral children and teenagers who enjoy soft drinks with an added 5 per cent alcohol content. Anyone who drinks the so-called alcopops such as Bacardi Breezer or Smirnoff Ice should be ignored, even if they happen to be your partner.

BRITISH PUBS

According to Sir Alex Ferguson, a good **pub** in the foreground can instantly improve the finest landscape in the world. A common stereotype of Great Britain is that it's a nation full of alcoholics. This is 99 per cent true, with the remaining 1 per cent being teetotalers.

What Government ministers call 'a binge-drinking crisis' many Britons would simply call 'Friday night'.

In every town around Great Britain there will be at least one public house. For many, this will be a second home, a place of refuge from all the other worries of the world around you. Friendly local hooligans may be able to enlighten you as to their whereabouts, other-wise just watch which direction the police head in at closing time.

When someone says 'Let's have a pint' they mean four or five. Similarly, going for 'a beer' means 'We are going to the pub and we prob-ably won't leave until closing time'.

Be aware of regulars. These are habitual customers of the pub, who might have their own favourite seat, special glass or their desperate eyes on the barmaid.

You will never get table service in a pub for drinks, although you might at the occasional wine bar. As a general rule, if you look at the drinks menu and think 'These prices must be for bottles not glasses' then you're getting table service.

'He never gets his round in.' There is no more damning assessment of one's character to be heard in the British Isles.

Pub Service

Things that will get you served faster:

- Being attractive.

- Knowing the bar staff.

- Being royal.

Things that will get you served slower:

- Being English (in Scotland).

- Being Scottish (in England).

- Being French (universal).

Anyone staying out late in the centre of London will witness a peculiar ritual as panicked locals swig down drinks, then run through the streets like Cinderella racing the chimes of midnight. This nightly curfew is set by the closure of the Underground. Trains are halted shortly after 12 a.m. to give maintenance crews a chance to attempt to clear eight years' worth of repairs in one night.

SPORT

It is common knowledge that Great Britain invented all sports. You name it, we invented it. The history of British sport is a long and painful story, encompassing the full scale of mediocrity and disappointment. The main driving point behind British sport is seeing how annoyed Australians get if and when we beat them.

Currently, the only British-invented sport in which we have a 100 per cent win rate is conkers.

In Wales the national sport is arguing. A Welshman takes great pride in his ability to argue with anyone for no apparent reason, even if secretly he agrees. Being from a different county/town/village/street/house/side of the bed is usually enough to guarantee a fight.

No matter what, the British are always on top of the imaginary Fair Play League. In fact, the phrase 'It's not the winning, it's the taking part' is now sewn on to our sports kits by law.

FOOTBALL

Football is the most popular sport in the world, loved by everyone except the Americans. The British are very passionate about it and it's easy to see why; who wouldn't want to spend ninety minutes watching a bunch of overpaid prima donnas chasing each other round a field, pretending to fall over and then going home to their ghastly orange-faced girlfriends? Matches in Britain are now seen around the world, meaning that up to 65 per cent of the world's population dislikes Adrian Chiles.

In 1966, England beat West Germany 4–2 (don't mention the score) at Wembley to win the World Cup. A feat we'll never repeat. Since that win, the England football team has gradually forgotten how to play successfully. The trophy room has been filled with wooden spoons and dust. Even the country's domestic cups are usually won by foreign teams, like Arsenal and Chelsea.

The England football team were 25/1 to win the World Cup 2014 in Brazil. For those who don't understand gambling, if you placed a bet of £10, you would've lost £10, after they managed to finish bottom in their qualifying group. Even the United States got further, and they don't even call it football. Carlsberg don't do football teams, they just sponsor them. But if they did, they'd still be better than England.

 Camilla says 'Rooney couldn't score in a brothel.' Although one seems to remember that's not entirely true.

Schoolboy football teams are now talking about making 'England-team errors'.

The only consolation the average football fan has is that however bad your team may be, it'll never be as bad as Scotland.

 FOR SALE: The England Football Team coach.
Low mileage, only used twice.

RUGBY

Picking up the football and running with it would normally earn you a thumping from the opposition, but for **William Webb Ellis** in 1823 it earned him the reputation as the inventor of an entirely new sport.

Rugby is a hooligan's sport, played by gentlemen. One team of fifteen players is sent on to the field to beat the living daylights out of the other team of fifteen players. There is a point system, but don't tell them that.

Like most sports invented by the British, it soon spread to other countries, and those other countries soon became much better at playing it. The bastards.

CRICKET

A sport that fills vast periods of time with vast amounts of waiting, pottering about and stopping for a cup of tea was always going to be popular with the British.

It is both the nation's summer game and a cause of bafflement for the rest of the world.

Cricket has some very slow moments, making it one of the few British sports where you can queue at the bar for twenty minutes without really missing much. It is currently the only game where you can actually put on weight whilst playing.

The first testicular safety guard was used in 1874 and the first safety helmet was used in

1974. It took exactly 100 years for men to realise that the brain is also an important part of the human anatomy.

HORSE RACING

Horse racing is the sport of kings that defies class.

Royal Ascot is the hoofed peak of the social season. It has become such a glamorous social event that coverage of people's attire far exceeds racing news. Visitors must obey a strict dress code: morning dress with top hat for gentlemen, whilst ladies must wear a dress that doesn't reveal too much flesh and a simple hat so as not to cause confusion with Princesses Beatrice and Eugenie.

Those who aren't situated within the Royal Enclosure should probably stay at home. This is the invitation-only area of the racecourse where high-ranked royals, Princess Anne with her 'dead-cert betting tips' and fame-hungry celebrities will be found.

The Peasants' Enclosure is full of silly old mares, and one isn't referring to the horses.

HORSE-RACE BETTING

There is no greater, and easier way, to get rich than by betting at the racecourse. Every year the bookies make an absolute fortune on which rare species of bird has been used to decorate Mummy's hat.

Carole and Michael Middleton are third in the coach procession at Ascot most of the time, which is a result, as one usually has them down as each way.

More than 500 million viewers worldwide tune in to watch their sweepstake pick crash into the first fence at the Grand National, the world's greatest steeplechase.

The Royal Family lost a small fortune betting on the race last year, although Cyprus wasn't worth that much to begin with.

One's Horse-racing Tips

- Point it in the right direction and tell it to run faster than the others.

- John McCririck will look like a tramp.

- Lunch Time 12–1.

- Happy Rambler – he'll walk it.

- Tesco Express.

- My Lidl Pony.

WIMBLEDON

Wimbledon is the annual 'Andy Murray – British or Scottish?' **tennis** tournament, officially sponsored by rain. The event provides a glorious fortnight of the British moaning about the weather, the price of strawberries and the country's consistent inability to produce tennis players that can get beyond the first round.

In the event of rain, the court will be covered to protect it. Viewers will be provided with earplugs to protect their ears from the warbling of Cliff Richard, which is usually only played to empty the court at the end of the day.

Some men watching women's tennis may not be totally focusing on the sport itself.

Andy Murray is a Scottish tennis player often regarded as grumpy and untalkative, although compared to the locals in his hometown he is a cheeky chatterbox. In 2013 he finally won the thing he's been dreaming about since childhood – British Citizenship.

He's very popular amongst the ladies, mainly his mother and girlfriend, who one feels sorry for, because to him love means nothing.

If he wins, he's British. If he loses, then he's back to being Scottish and sponsored by Pritt Stick – great on paper, rubbish on any other surface.

One's not entirely bothered with the lack of British wins, because with strawberries at £5 each, we're making all that prize money back.

FISHING

Fishing is an extremely popular pastime amongst British men who would rather sit on the side of a river in the pissing rain than be at home with their wives and families.

OLYMPICS

It wouldn't be right or very British of one to not mention the pride, pomp and circumstance that featured during the **London 2012 Olympics**.

More than 1 billion viewers worldwide
watched the opening ceremony, with performances celebrating Britain's history and
culture. **David Beckham** was sent to Athens,
Greece, to collect the Olympic Torch, but he
blew it out on the way back after thinking it
was a birthday candle. Idiot.

One's favourite part of the opening ceremony
was the flag parade showing all the countries
we've conquered. The most remembered part
was Mother parachuting 1,000 feet from a
helicopter with James Bond, although you'd
have to be a complete idiot to think she actually jumped. She was pushed.

The European countries were all hoping
to do well in the Olympics, as they wanted
to melt their medals down to help boost
their economies.

In true competitive spirit, the British set off with
their stiff upper lip to outrun the competition.

For the spectators there was the prospect of watching a lot of sweaty people trying to get from A to B in the shortest time possible – not much different to the normal commute to work on a Monday morning. Starting pistols were banned as they confused the French competitors, making them run in the wrong direction.

Not long after the start of the Olympics, Greece was already sixteen medals in debt. They eventually managed to win something, but were slightly disappointed that there's no such thing as 'Cash my bronze'.

The ticket-allocation system operated in such a way as to prevent anybody, except for **Lord Coe**, from getting the tickets.

Super Saturday refers to Day 8 when Great Britain recorded their most successful medal haul in a day at the Olympics for 104 years. It was Team GB's greatest day in sporting history, yet we still lost on penalties.

The 2012 Olympics cost over £9 billion, which is a lot of money and bankrupted London. But you simply can't put a price on eight gold medals in cycling. Five million people attended Olympic events, making it the second biggest attraction after the Job Centre.

Great Britain won a total of 65 medals. The Empire Strikes Back.

 If you're wondering why the British are so good at cycling and rowing, take a look at the cost of public transport.

Cheering on the Underdog

As a nation of animal lovers, our favourite creature is probably the **underdog**. A Briton watching a sport with no preference for a team or player will naturally support the weakest one. We watch the Eurovision Song Contest just to cheer on whichever nation is collecting the most 'nil points', although, of course, that's usually us ...

CHAPTER 5

Daily Life

Predominantly there are two things the British public like doing more than anything else: moaning and queueing.

This chapter could not have been possible without helpful insight from the Middleton family, who prior to promotion to Royal Family status have spent many years within modern-day Britain.

GETTING AROUND THE UK

Visitors will be struck by the frequency with which conversation in the British Isles will turn to the dire state of the nation's public transportation system. The ultimate icebreaker is achieved by announcing your apologies for being late, even if you're quite punctual, and blaming it on the bus, train or traffic.

CARS

Driving around the UK should not be attempted unless you have one, preferably both, of the following:

1 A Bentley, Rolls-Royce, or an eight-horse-drawn solid-gold carriage.

2 A chauffeur.

Unlike most countries, the British drive on the left-hand side of the road, but don't be daunted. Most roads are so narrow that it doesn't make any difference which side you're on.

To park your car for an hour in Britain costs more than the minimum wage. People working in shops can look out of the window and see parking meters earning more than they do.

The London congestion charge is a scheme implemented with the stated goal of reducing traffic and carbon emissions. It has done neither. To queue or not to queue; that is congestion. No one is exempt from this fine, not even you, President Obama. One is still waiting for payment, plus interest.

BUSES

Covering approximately 32,000 square miles, London buses are the world's largest collection of red paint. Unfortunately, not many buses are actually red nowadays, as they're plastered in adverts for sodding awful films. There are 673 routes, all having a contractual obligation to run down Oxford Street whilst roadworks are occurring.

London's big red buses are one of the greatest and most recognisable icons of Great Britain. Like Britain itself, everyone tries to squeeze on for a free ride and ends up going nowhere.

SHOPPING

ARGOS

Argos is essentially a British catalogue store comparable to Internet shopping without the Internet, where customers are no more than twenty days away from being served. Customers are able to check the availability of products by using a special computerised system, which is almost guaranteed to tell you that the product is out of stock.

HARRODS

Harrods is an overpriced department store in the heart of London, which has become a desirable brand in its own right. A Harrods carrier bag suggests that its owner may be worth mugging. As well as being a supplier of the finest luxury items required in life, it also has the ability to perform open-wallet surgery by turning everyday necessities into expensive treats. The staff famously brag that 'Harrods sells everything', but the fact you still can't buy a new Prime Minister is a definite oversight.

MARKS & SPENCER
M&S is a store where literally everyone in Britain buys their socks and underwear. Camilla has apparently seen Samantha Cameron buying thongs in there, or dental floss as she calls them. You are fully expected to care greatly about the fortunes of this over-priced store. When this store falls, so does Britain. Their promotional advert states that it wouldn't be Christmas without M&S. They're right too. It would be Chrita.

TESCO
Tesco is a large supermarket chain, which one suspects recruits staff by waiting outside school gates for the eventual dropouts.

Foodstuff and unwanted bin-bottom scrapings are cruelly moulded into products known as

'Tesco Everyday Value', allowing the lower classes of society to live the life of luxury thanks to high-street retail. It is only whilst spending hours on the toilet that reality kicks in.

The news in January 2013 that Tesco had been selling 'beef burgers' containing up to 28 per cent horse meat was met unenthusiastically by the public, although to be fair, one didn't realise there was that much meat in them anyway. No wonder the Middletons' barbecue gave one the trots. Low in fat, high in Shergar. When your daughter asks for a pony for her birthday, it often works to simply buy her a Tesco Quarter Pounder.

IKEA

IKEA is a large Swedish imported store, which makes millions of pounds by tricking the customers into thinking it's good to have to build their own furniture. Having decided which of the billions of items sold by IKEA it is that you wish to buy, you will need to visit your local store, which is at least 80 miles away. For some shoppers it is impossible to visit their store without wanting to actually live there.

Management confirmed that traces of horse meat were also found in their Swedish meatballs, popularly served in their restaurants. One would've been more shocked if they found wood in their furniture.

 Have you overspent during your visit? Pop into a Jobcentre Plus who, after a few basic questions, will happily refund the rest of your stay.

RESTAURANTS
MCDONALD'S
McDonald's is a chain of fast-food restaurants famed for ingraining the staple diet of America into British society with products such as the Big Mac, although quite frankly

one has seen more meat on a butcher's
pencil.

STARBUCKS
Yes, there's a **Starbucks** on every street
corner, but they're just for the tourists. Coffee
isn't one's cup of tea, nor is it any good.

COSTA COFFEE
The official competitor of Starbucks is **Costa
Coffee** – same crap, different place.

HOTELS
Visitors to British hotels will soon realise that,
contrary to popular belief, *Fawlty Towers* was
actually a documentary. There is an abundance of
hotels where you can book a room for the night.
These include Travelodge and Premier Inn,
where everything is premier, except the inn.

Visitors will note the almost mandatory provi-
sion of an electric kettle in every hotel room.

When you see the words **'Bed and Breakfast'** or **'B+B'** outside a hotel, you know you are guaranteed two things: a bed and, occasionally, a breakfast. Breakfast will have carefully been selected from a vast array of local suppliers, though this is because the eggs are cheapest at Asda, the bacon at Lidl and the sausages at Iceland.

Those who want to look and smell nice must have time to crack the Enigma code in order to use the showers located in the hotel bathroom.

DAILY COMMUTE

The correct demeanour to effect when commuting to work is **subdued glumness**. No visible signs of happiness or contentment should ever tarnish one's face, until three hours have been spent in your workplace, which took more than four hours to get to.

If this sounds a little unfriendly, you are completely misunderstanding a key part of the

British psyche. That's because commuting is only part of the psychical voyage. The far more important journey being undertaken is the psychological alteration from being 'at home' as opposed to being 'at work'. During this process, no form of social interaction should be attempted. Should you want to blend into British society, you should learn to do the same. And whatever you do, **don't smile**. Ever.

If you're worried about the commute to work being unsettled by predicted snow, patchy rain or tube strikes, you can always download a travel update app on to your phone. Or Facebook, as it's also known.

Sunday travel – don't, just don't.

LONDON UNDERGROUND

London Underground is a role-playing game played by millions of people every day beneath the streets of London. 'Commuters' (as game participants are called) have to battle their way through the crowds to reach their destination.

Various obstacles are thrown in by the Underground staff to make the game more difficult and challenging for the player. These include:

- Trains breaking down.

- Trains arriving up to half an hour late without an apology or explanation.

- Fines for having the wrong ticket.

- Employees going on strike and shutting the place down because they feel that £50k is not enough to sit on their arse all day.

High-priced paper tickets can be bought at stations, but have been made more or less obsolete by a cheaper electronic service

known as **Oyster**, probably named this
because the price of travel makes you gag
when swallowed whole. Tickets are quite
expensive, but you can save money by booking
eight or nine years in advance. The renewal of
your monthly or weekly season ticket should
be purchased on the actual day of travel to
ensure formation of an enormous queue.

The Underground network is actually mostly
overground and stretches from the heart of the
city to the fringes of the countryside. You can
ride north on the Piccadilly line to Cockfosters,
simply to snigger at the name, or you can travel
out to Heathrow Airport in marginally less time
than it takes to fly to Shanghai.

Travellers are advised to take a deep breath
upon entering the trains, as no fresh air will
be available until they reach street level again.

When riding escalators, the only meaningful
test of Britishness is knowing to **stand on the**

right. Standing still on the left of the escalator will result in death within seconds, if not by stampede, then by verbal abuse. Be warned.

Waiting for the train should take place at the exact same spot on the platform every morning and evening. It is a tradition that trains generally do not run on time unless the passenger is two minutes late.

Doors will open automatically. Never press the 'Open' button. This doesn't function and is merely there to humiliate visitors and give passengers something to laugh at when Cockfosters starts to wear thin.

 Been for a ride on the Tube to celebrate 150 years of London Underground. Or if you count strikes, 20 years.

Patrons are advised that the average temperature inside the carriages is 34 degrees Celsius throughout the year; so take a plentiful supply of water, and if possible a portable shower.

Statistics show Londoners can spend up to eighteen months of their lives commuting. That's the Northern line for you.

If you manage to arrive at your stop without being hassled by a busker or having your pockets picked, you have done extremely well. To avoid pickpockets when travelling, simply replace the contents of your pockets with euros.

A lot of people criticise London Underground, but without doubt, we have the finest rail replacement network in the whole of Europe. Having survived the Blitz, the 2005 terrorist attacks and 14,326 busker renditions of 'American Pie', the London Underground is still going strong. It may be the most efficient and expensive way of making yourself late in history, but having

been around for 150 years, for all its faults,
demands and ...

Oh, forget it. One suggests you get on a bus
or 'borrow' a bicycle from Boris instead.

THE BRITISH CLASS SYSTEM

The **British class system** is complex; so
complex that even the British don't fully
understand it and will spend days debating
which class they are in. Whether you are a
lord, a lady or just the king of your own
middle-class kingdom, everyone in the British
Isles fits into the class system.

Some class barriers have broken down; otherwise one wouldn't be sitting here writing this
section. Other countries eradicated their own
class systems by rounding up the upper
classes and beheading them.

If there's one thing one simply cannot stand
it's snobbism. People who pretend they're

superior make it harder for those of us who really are.

Jumping class boundaries is extremely difficult: moving from working to middle means acquiring a taste for olives and houmous; whilst moving from middle to upper means knowing which fork goes where and which servant should polish them.

WORKING CLASS

The **working class** used to be those that worked for a living. Now, the working class are the only class that don't actually work at all; instead they have the unusual career of 'being on the dole', at no fault of their own. Poor sods.

Favourite TV programme: *Only Fools and Horses*.

Favourite food: Takeaway.

Favourite drink: Cups of tea, as it helps make their situation bearable for five minutes.

MIDDLE CLASS

This group no longer has its own identity and heritage, but is now sandwiched between the working and upper classes. Education counts for a lot less with the **middle class** as literacy skills are measured by the amount of outrage expressed whilst reading a copy of the *Daily Mail*.

Coming from all walks of life, they have worked and saved to rise above their humble beginnings and gain the coveted status of 'Rich Gits'. Once there, they can attempt to intermingle themselves into the higher society, despite still being relatively 'rough around the edges'.

Favourite TV programme: *Question Time* – which is *The Jeremy Kyle Show* for the middle class.

Favourite food: Anything from within two certain sections of Waitrose: organic and things you can afford.

Favourite drink: Disaronno – making the middle class feel upper class since 1525.

UPPER CLASS

The British **upper class** is not just a class. It is in fact a distinct species; a species that has existed in Britain for thousands of years. In that time not one drop of upper-class blood has mixed with that of the lower classes. Sadly, their inability to breed with the lower classes has led to a decline in the genetic pool.

If there is one thing that separates rich from poor, it's money. And that is a shame, because there should really be much more separating the rich from the poor than just one thing.

Favourite TV programme: *University Challenge*.

Favourite food: Truffles, caviar.

Favourite drink: Gin and Dubonnet.

BRITISH WEATHER

If there's one thing that makes the British people almost instantly recognisable, it's their obsession with the current **weather**. British weather is exactly like the British Government – always wrong.

Great Britain is the only country where it can rain all summer, yet the Government still enforces a hosepipe ban. You know you're in a bloody damp country when the slightest hint of sunshine is front-page news. It is a testament to British genius that we have managed to make our very moderate, delicately nuanced weather a subject of national conversation.

Britain has four seasons. Whilst the transformation between them can be pleasant, each is typically as wet, grey and cold as the last. By the way, 'wet, grey and cold' are all considered to be ice-cream weather.

A scattering of snow brings the country to a complete stop and a little less rain than usual starts a drought, sending the Government into a hosepipe-banning meltdown. The rail network is particularly vulnerable to weather – trains have been cancelled for everything from leaves on the track to the wrong type of snow. In short, Great Britain is the only nation that runs more efficiently through a world war than a snowstorm.

Umbrellas

The United Kingdom is the leading global market for **umbrellas.** Approximately 450,000 umbrellas are left on public transport during June and July (summer). Lost-property staff hoping to reunite the umbrellas with their owners tend to seek a slightly more accurate description than 'It was a black one'.

Although we complain bitterly about the weather, the British remain optimistic about the chances of it changing. Where a glimmer of sun passes unnoticed in most places, we greet it with exposed gin bellies and bikinis.

Prince Harry must be coated from head to toe in suntan lotion (volunteers needed – apply within) as he burns easily, especially when he sunbathes naked. Prince William on the other hand is slightly more reserved than his brother. His Union Jack mankini covers his pride, but causes awful tan lines.

THE WEATHER FORECAST

Sky TV has a channel dedicated to Britain's weather – that's right, twenty-four hours of **weather forecasting**. One has something similar to that in Clarence House – it's called a sodding window.

The BBC weather bulletins are amongst the most accurate in the UK, with a success rating almost reaching 1 per cent. This statistic has been achieved by covering up half of the country with large weather symbols, allowing the BBC to argue the weather was always right somewhere.

'Earlier on today, apparently, a woman rang the BBC and said she heard there was a hurricane on the way; well, if you're watching, don't worry, there isn't.'

So said weatherman Michael Fish on the evening before the Great Storm of 1987, which took out 15 million trees and cost an estimated £18 billion to clear up. Camilla says 'He couldn't predict a riot if he listened to the Kaiser Chiefs', and quite frankly one agrees. One can confirm that Mr Fish will stop paying compensation towards his hurricane inaccuracy shortly after the world implodes.

Back in 2012, one did a live weather forecast for the BBC: scattered sunshine, with a minimal chance of reign. The footage went viral around the world. Mother hates being upstaged, so she took Father to the *Antiques Roadshow* for a valuation.

HOLIDAYS

Once a year most British families take an extended **holiday**. If you look like your passport photo, then in all probability you need the holiday. Until air travel became more common, family holidays were almost always spent in one of the many British **seaside resorts**. Foreign holidays are occasionally acceptable, but fully expect to return home with diarrhoea, food poisoning and to be told 'You've caught the sun', indicating you're burnt to a crisp.

Great Britain has a lot of coastline, more than 7,000 miles of it. Seaside resorts are a British institution, where even the poorest of subjects can have their very own castle – made from sand. It is the place to go to enjoy melting ice creams, ride flea-ridden donkeys on the beach and catch crabs.

A common sight on the shoreline of many British seaside towns is that of a **beach hut**. These small, brightly coloured, wooden boxes, usually displaying a large rusty padlock, are simply nothing more than a garden shed. They are generally used as a shelter from the sun (once in a blue moon), wind (more often) and rain (most likely); for changing into swimming costumes; and for the safe storing of beach paraphernalia. Deckchairs, windbreaks, camping stoves, chipped mugs, flip-flops and inflatable balls are neatly stored inside, ready and waiting for the next sunny day at the beach – which would explain the rusty padlock.

The two most popular piers that Britain has to offer are **Brighton** and **Southend**, with the least popular being Morgan.

Blackpool

Blackpool is located in north-west England and is generally considered to have been the inspiration for Las Vegas. This number-one seaside resort clocks up more visitors than anywhere else in the UK, despite the fact that the sewage there is cleaner than the sea. Being a popular destination for stag and hen dos alike, Blackpool is still in a post-'999 What's your emergency?' hangover.

Tourists flock to the seaside resort to climb the famous **Blackpool Tower** and admire its views (some say they can see as far as WHSmith on Bank Hey Street).

The local amusement park, known as the **Pleasure Beach**, is a popular destination for those tourists who don't mind if the brakes on Europe's tallest and fastest roller coaster are a sturdy pair of steel-toed boots on the feet of a spotty teenaged ride attendant.

CARAVANNING

Couples, who fancy testing their marriage vows by pushing themselves to the absolute brink, can spend a week shed dragging – or as it's more commonly known, **caravanning**. British families spend days on end appearing to enjoy leaking Thermos flasks, chemical toilets, gnat bites and cold showers every morning. With absolutely no way to escape each other, if your marriage vows can survive sleeping inside something that resembles a tin can, it can survive anything. As Camilla says, 'If the caravan's a-rockin', don't come a-knockin''.

 The saying goes that 'All roads lead to Rome'. This certainly isn't true in the case of the M4. One drove along it and ended up in Swindon.

BRITISH ETIQUETTE

From addressing an envelope to addressing the Queen, proper **etiquette** is needed for all of life's events, big and small. Etiquette should most definitely *not* be confused with manners. Manners involve general behavioural guidelines that can be picked up through even the scrappiest of upbringings. British etiquette, on the other hand, is a specific **code of behaviour** that encompasses most aspects of social interaction in society. In short, the more the British dislike you, the more polite they are.

In British society, there are very strict rules on conduct, especially on how and when you should greet your fellow Britons. With enough teaching and guidance, even the most untrained creatures can bluff the simple rules featured in the *British Book of Etiquette*, which the Middleton family have been writing and updating since 2010.

The *American Book of Etiquette* happens to be a very slim volume.

Saying Hello

There are many ways in which a British person can say **hello.** It's an extraordinarily familiar greeting, one you should never, under any circumstances, use on any member of the Royal Family should they visit your town (see box on page 192). Subjects who use this informal introduction on the Queen can expect a firm slap round the chops, as Leslie Phillips found out whilst receiving his CBE.

'All right?'

This is 'Hello' and 'How are you?' all in one. It is used when you really can't be bothered to say hello with any enthusiasm because you're greeting someone you see every day, and whilst you are pleased to see them, the reason you are seeing them is because you're both arriving at some mutual obligation, like a workplace or school. Or you're both naturally quite dry people. The normal response would be for them to say the same back to you, whilst giving a slight nod of the head.

'Ay-up'

An inquisitory hello that carries an assumption that there is a pressing matter needing to be discussed as soon as the pleasantries are out of the way.

'Wotcha'

When you're meeting someone, often the thing you want to ask is how they are doing. You can jump straight in by enquiring as to their health and general wellbeing, or if you are feeling less formal, you can go for this slang term that effectively means the same thing. 'Wotcha' is a mush-mouthed degradation of 'What cheer be with you?', which effectively asks if you've got any news, good or otherwise. Not to be used by anyone who isn't a complete tosser.

HANDSHAKE

Like much of the world, in Britain a **firm handshake** lasting a few seconds is the common form of face-to-face greeting for all business situations and most social meetings too. Always use your right hand, and shake firmly. Be careful not to accidentally rearrange their bone structure by squeezing their hand with a machine-like grip.

Not quite catching someone's name means you can never speak to him or her again. Thankfully this worked out well with whatshisface from Take That.

Meet the Family

If you are lucky enough to be invited to meet members of the Royal Family, keep in mind the following **rules of protocol** to avoid committing crimes that could haunt you for years to come whilst imprisoned in the Tower of London:

• When you meet Mother or other female members of the Royal Family for the first time you should address them as 'Your Majesty' or 'Your Royal Highness' respectively. From then on use 'Ma'am', as in 'ham', not 'Ma'am' as in 'farm'. For male members of the Royal Family, use 'Your Royal Highness' and subsequently 'Sir'.

• Don't say 'Pleased to meet you', because quite frankly that's bloody obvious.

• High-fiving, winking, chewing gum, showing off your tattoos and big bearhugs are inappropriate.

Ps and Qs

The first rule that British subjects come across at an early age is **'Mind your Ps and Qs'**, which has absolutely nothing to do with waiting politely to use the toilet.

This vital piece of advice has been customary in Britain as an abbreviation of 'to mind your manners', or more specifically to say both 'please' (Ps) and 'thank you' (thank-Qs). It is almost a certainty that parents will grow weary of the repetition of 'Say please/thank you' every few minutes for the first five, six or fifteen years of their child's existence. A child who isn't constantly reminded about their Ps and Qs, the most basic of good manners, is being given a very poor start in life, especially in a British society, and will most likely end up served with an ASBO as they grow older.

The British have to show a considerable amount of restraint to thank the waiter clearing each item from their table, in order to deliver a massive 'Thank you' at the end.

Stiff Upper Lip

One of the great British characteristics, the **stiff upper lip**, was obtained by 'Sucking on Viagra instead of swallowing it' as the Queen Mother, God rest her soul, used to say. It refers to a very British stoicism that manages to treat issues of great seriousness as if they are utterly trivial. During times of war, the stiff upper lips have held us together as a nation.

British subjects are always expected to 'Keep a stiff upper lip regardless', a piece of advice that one simply cannot imagine in any accent other than a British one.

Americans, on the other hand, have surgically enhanced Botoxed upper lips.

Moaning

The British love to complain, but are rubbish at doing it. In order to loosen our stiff upper lip a good **moan** about anything that springs to mind is essential. Quite simply, there's nothing we enjoy more than moaning about a whole range of subjects from bad backs to the idiots ruining the country, often causing the moaning swingometer to explode.

Tutting

For the vast majority of Brits, **tutting** is the noise you make when your bus is late, you're queueing behind an elderly lady at a super-market paying with every coin known to mankind or you're being mistaken for an Australian by an American.

Made by sucking the tip of your tongue away from your teeth through pursed lips, the sound is best served with rolled eyes, whilst mentally repeating the word 'Typical'. This was precisely Winston Churchill's reaction when the French forces waved their white handkerchiefs at the advancing German army during the Second World War.

APOLOGISING

One is sorry to have to bring this up, but the British are apologetic to the point of irritation. If you spend any time in the UK you're bound to have someone tell you they're sorry. If the British could make anything other than queueing an international sport, then it would be **apologising**. We're so good at it that we do it even when we don't need to. Brits are sorry for practically everything. We're sorry when you bump into us in the street, when we can't hear what you're saying or when you tread on our toes. Unless, of course, it happens to be the foot of a royal, in which case you'll be arrested and taken to the Tower by your short and curlies.

The simple act of saying sorry is often regarded as the hardest word to say, but in one's humble opinion that's the name of that Welsh railway station.

TIPPING

To tip or not to tip, that is the question. Paying gratuity has been a British custom since the Tudor dynasty. Henry VIII gave a tip to his servants to 'Put more food on his plate in future', which judging by the size of the sod they quite obviously did.

The average tip is £4.72, plus a couple of euros, although don't use tipping as an excuse to offload a pocketful of coppers, small change or a gentleman's shirt button. British restaurants love American customers. This is because the customary tip in the United States is around twice what it is in the UK.

A Handy Guide to the Distant Art of British Tipping

- Barstaff: Not expected unless table service is provided. You can politely offer to buy them a drink. If they accept, you could get lucky; if they refuse, you haven't lost anything. It's a win-win situation.

- Hairdresser/barber: Rate your newly trimmed sex appeal out of 10, divide by 2. For example, a rating of 8 divided by 2 = £4 tip. If your sex-appeal rating is less than before you walked in, then leave without paying.

- Taxi: Calculate the number of air fresh-eners necessary to counterbalance the smell you're leaving behind. Provide extra cash to cover the cost.

QUEUEING

The absolute giveaway to British national identity is the ability to form an **orderly queue** with just two people. We are born with the ability to queue. If a person stands still for more than one minute, then another will be drawn to line up behind them.

When we see other people standing one behind the other, slowly shuffling forward, we are powerless to resist and must join them, regardless of the fact that we have no idea what the queue is for or where it's going. If queueing ever became an Olympic sport, Britain would undoubtedly win gold every time.

If two people arrive at the same time, you can always spot the Brit. They'll be the one who says 'After you'.

It is very easy to underestimate how seriously we take this business. It really is a matter of life and death. In fact, one reason why more British people died during the *Titanic* disaster is because the Brits queued for the lifeboats, whereas others did not.

If you are nervous about joining in this national pastime, then here are a few basic rules to help you:

1 **No pushing in.** This is the cardinal rule. Ignoring the huge line of dull-faced people is enough to get you deported from the British Isles. Many people think Piers Morgan moved to the USA of his own accord, but in reality he pushed to the front of a queue of twelve at a petrol station on the M4 and had to flee the country for his own safety. The back of the queue will be easy to spot, as it will be the end where you are confronted with a fellow queuer's arse. If you join the queue and are confronted by another person's angry face,

then you have inadvertently joined the front of the queue.

2   **Keep close formation.** Leave no gaps between you and the person in front as these can be seen as an invitation to the opportunistic queue jumper. At no point should there ever be enough space for a full place to be taken. It's all about constant shuffling, as though your feet are glued to the person in front.

3   **Sob stories** only work on employees in customer-service departments who haven't been stood in the queue for three hours. You have a flight to catch? Then you should have been there four days early like everyone else.

4   The **other queue** always moves faster.

ETIQUETTE TIPS FOR LADIES

Upon being introduced to a gentleman, a lady should never offer her hand, but instead should bow politely and say 'I am happy to make your acquaintance', whilst slipping her business card into one of the pockets of his suit. A lady does not leave her card plastered to the sides of telephone boxes.

If one cannot sit in a ladylike manner, this guidebook may at least preserve one's modesty.

Ball gowns should be of delicate, flimsy material, though not so flimsy as to be rendered transparent by bright light – unless one is in the company of Prince Andrew.

ETIQUETTE TIPS FOR GENTLEMEN

A gentleman will always tip his hat to greet a lady. It is not customary to greet her by squeezing both breasts twice and simultaneously shouting, 'Honk honk'.

Winking should be reserved for women of the lower classes.

Men may kiss women in greeting, but be careful if you decide to kiss on both cheeks. If a woman is only expecting one kiss they may not turn their head for the second and will receive it full-frontally, which can result in the worst being feared. During the reinstallation of President Obama, one witnessed Prince Philip accidentally snog Hillary Clinton, even though Mother thinks of it as deliberate.

CHAPTER 6

Capital Cities

LONDON, ENGLAND

London, the great central city of the universe, features a diverse range of cultures. More than 300 languages are spoken within its boundaries, most of which are used to talk about the people from the other cultures without suspicion.

The **River Thames** flows through the centre of the city. It currently holds the record as the most polluted river in the world and famously causes odd smells, daily at 4 p.m.

London is home to the beloved **Cockneys**. According to tradition, to be a Cockney you have to be born within the sound of Bow Bells. Although, technically, no Cockney has been born since 1945 as the Germans bombed the church out of existence during the Second World War.

The best way to get around London is to hitch a ride with a taxi driver, who'll drive as though they are being chased by the rear seats of the cab. To pay the fare you'll need to remortgage your house, but then you'll never be able to afford a house in London anyway.

Under no circumstances should you remain silent throughout your journey. You are fully expected to ask your taxi driver if they have had a busy day.

Alternatively, you could use London's bike-hire scheme, introduced by **Mayor Boris Johnson**, which is simpler than the man himself. Just go up to the terminal at any docking station, pay by card and take away one of the so-called 'Boris bikes'. When you've spent twenty minutes trying to get it to move, simply throw it into the nearest canal, as they're absolutely sodding useless.

The UK has created a whole network of cycle lanes; these are marked with two yellow lines and can be used in any direction.

THINGS TO DO

The **British Museum** is the largest museum in the UK. If you do manage to visit all the endless sections of historical interest, archaeologists will simply dig up the bones of another 15th-century king from under a car park just to annoy you.

Possibly the most famous clock face and chimes in the world, **Big Ben** is actually the name of the largest bell (13.5 tons) in Britain, which hangs inside the Elizabeth Tower. The second-largest bell (14 stone) sits in the main offices of Number 10 Downing Street.

Members of Parliament on their lunch breaks like to stroll round the square near Big Ben. Anything to pass the time.

Madame Tussauds is a museum for tourists who like to pose with major historical figures, actors, singers, sportspeople and self-absorbed idiots replicated in wax.

The members of One Direction are the latest celebrities to have realistic replica Tussauds waxwork figures made of themselves. The five models are exactly identical to the band, including their inability to sing. After the recent downturn in his career, George Michael has taken a minimum-wage job imitating his own waxwork.

If you decide against visiting Madame Tussauds, you can easily fool people into thinking you've been by having your photo taken with various celebrities.

EDINBURGH, SCOTLAND
(Please ignore if they voted 'AYE' for independence.)

Scotland, the loft extension of England, has

provided the world with many great inventions over the years, including the television, the sporran and Sean Connery. Contrary to popular belief, Mel Gibson is not Scottish. The list of things invented by the Scots grows directly in proportion to the amount of alcohol consumed. If they are allowed access to more than three bottles, they'll apparently have invented everything.

Scotland's primary export is wind. On a particularly breezy day in the tenth century, Lord Lothian had arrived to officially declare the newest lowland city of Edin open for business. A strong gust of wind blew from the east at exactly the right moment. Edin-burrrrrgh was born.

You wouldn't think **Edinburgh** was one of the top ten holiday destinations in Europe – and you would be right. Despite this, the city still attracts millions of visitors every year. This is mainly due to the unique time warp that affects the area, which causes the city to remain in the Middle Ages. Edinburgh should be visited by everybody at least once in their life. After visiting, leave it ten years, then visit again, just to see how little it has changed.

As you start exploring the cobbled streets, you may start to hear what sounds like someone strangling a cat. This is none other than the sound of Scotland's famous bagpipes, which were given to them years before as a prank by the Irish. Unfortunately, the Scots haven't got the joke yet.

Tartan is the fabric of Scotland's national costume, with everyone wearing kilts of their clan's tartan. The people of Essex have their own tartan; this is called Burberry. One has a direct method of telling which clan a Scotsman belongs to; if you reach your hand up his kilt and feel a quarter pounder, he's almost certainly a McDonald.

THINGS TO DO

Edinburgh Castle was built by King David I of Scotland in 1130 as a gift for his consort, Matilda. It was designed to be a carbon copy of Windsor Castle, however, due to a mathematical balls-up it was only half the size. Matilda didn't particularly like it, but at the end of the day, it's the fort that counts.

You can still see various crumbling sections of **Hadrian's Wall**, which is currently being rebuilt along the border between Scotland and England in time for their expected vote of independence.

CARDIFF, WALES

Wales, commonly referred to as 'the buttocks of Britain', has many areas of outstanding natural beauty: the Anglesey coast, the mountains of Snowdonia, the flocking sheep, Katherine Jenkins and the eastward drive over the Severn Bridge, which is free if you're travelling in the right direction.

The beauty of the Welsh landscape attracts many tourists to the country each year. In an effort to avoid this, the Welsh Government passed a law to remove over 65 per cent of all vowels used in the place names of its towns and villages. If you enjoy sitting in a caravan watching television with a bad signal, whilst your partner complains about the weather, then Wales is the perfect destination.

Royal tour of Wales. Thought one was visiting a town called Llanthwgcyrigabreth before realising the tour guide had a hair in his mouth.

In the seventeenth century Wales was used as a prison by the English. No chains or walls were needed as no one could read the signs, so any potential escapee got lost within two minutes. The longest town name has been omitted from this guidebook, simply due to the fear of running out of space.

THINGS TO DO

Despite one technically being the Prince of Wales, one can't lie to you – there is literally nothing to do in the Welsh Valleys, unless you're a big fan of sheep.

The **Motorpoint Arena Cardiff** is a great venue if you want to watch your favourite bands play in possibly the worst venue in Britain and half suffocate in the process. If you enjoy your live music loud and a muddy mess of sound, then this is definitely the ideal place to go.

BELFAST, NORTHERN IRELAND

Northern Ireland was often forgotten about and ignored by the other nations comprising the United Kingdom, until they beat the England football team in 2005, reminding everyone of their existence. It is the only part of Britain that shares a border with a foreign country, the Republic of Ireland (working title).

Contrary to popular belief, Northern Ireland is not full of alcoholics; some people are in fact sober (mostly children). God created alcohol just to stop the Irish from ruling the world.

THINGS TO DO

Belfast Central Library is world renowned for being the only library in the world that has more staff than books.

The **Titanic Belfast** is one of the largest and most well-thought-out museums in the world. It gives customers the chance to witness the large, empty structure known as the Irish birthplace of the so-called 'unsinkable ship', a nickname that was apparently made up by someone who'd never heard of Sod's Law. Visitors expecting to see memorabilia from the ship will be disappointed, as due to unforeseen circumstances the items of interest are currently resting 12,000 feet below the Atlantic Ocean.

CHAPTER 7

The Best of British

FULL ENGLISH BREAKFAST

Breakfast. The full English. The full monty. A fry-up. Call it what you want, but there are few nations in this world that do breakfast better than the British. The breakfast of champions is the most important meal of the day, so naturally it should set the standard in terms of health and nutrition. The concept is simple: get the majority of your calories in at the beginning of the day to keep you productive and content until you can get home from the office, field or factory. Delivering a power-packed 465,873 calories, a full English breakfast blows the foreign continental breakfast of a croissant, a piece of fruit and a glass of juice clean out of the English Channel.

Tourists enjoy the traditional English breakfast because they don't often eat such things at home. If they did, they would die. It simply isn't in their DNA.

The single most important ingredient for any breakfast claiming to be the full English is **bacon**. These greasy slices of pig are the artery-hardening heart of any good breakfast.

Of course, we don't just want to enjoy the backs and bellies of our swinely companions. We want to enjoy all that they have to offer. In one meaty little package a **sausage** can offer up the piggy delights that we would otherwise have to chew through trotters and snouts for. Bacon aside, breakfast provides no finer delights than this minced-gristle offering. As an added bonus, it comes wrapped in delicious hog intestines for extra porky goodness. The British love a meaty banger.

If anything about our mighty breakfast repre-sents the blood of our fine nation, it's **black pudding**. You've already enjoyed 90 per cent of the pig, how could you even consider letting the lovely thick blood go to waste?

Is it really a full English without a **hash brown**? No.

Fried egg is the only option for this type of breakfast. You've come so far, so why ruin it now? Of course, it is acceptable to have scrambled eggs, but only if you are seven years old.

As everybody no doubt knows, **baked beans** are the musical fruit. These will provide the fanfare in celebration of your real Briton's breakfast.

Margarine is a French invention. Enough said. But the spreading of full-fat butter on bread is a complete waste. If you're a real Brit, then you'll know that a **fried slice** is the perfect accompaniment to any breakfast. It's the greatest invention since un-fried bread.

Now, sit back, stir two sugars into your tea and enjoy. Eat it all up for England, St George and one's mother.

FISH AND CHIPS

Friday. **Fish and chips.** A national institution that sustained morale through two world wars and helped fuel Britain's industrial prime. Like Morecambe and Wise, ~~Cameron and Clegg~~ and Wallace and Gromit, fish and chips are a classic double act – and yet they started life as solo performers.

One doesn't know who came up with the idea of putting fish and chips together, but they certainly look good on paper.

One doesn't take anything seriously in the newspaper, except for fish and chips. And even that one takes with a pinch of salt.

The Food Standards Agency has recently instructed vendors to sell 'cod and chips' rather than 'fish and chips', because they have nothing better to do with their time.

CUP OF TEA

The Spanish have siestas, the French have affairs, but the British have the **cup of tea.**

Originally discovered by chimps wearing human clothes, the appreciation for an afternoon cup of tea remains an entrenched part of Great Britishness. Much like the weather, it cuts to the very core of what it is to be British and is sewn into our cultural identity.

A warm, comforting cup of tea is Britain's soul food, with the accompaniment of at least four biscuits being your patriotic, legal duty. It is a universal truth that the ultimate feeling of sorrow is experienced upon discovery of a forgotten cup of tea.

If you're a British citizen, and don't like tea, one strongly advises you to see your doctor immediately. If you're not a tea lover (shame on you), one seriously suggests you pretend to be one.

Whether it's a family crisis, a medical emergency, a government scandal or an international emergency, sitting down with a cup of tea is an almost guaranteed way of solving problems or at least making things a little less severe. Just the other day one sat down with Pope Francis over a cup of tea and Chocolate Hobnobs (his favourite biscuit), discussing everything from world peace, global warming and Freddie Mercury becoming a saint, to who has the biggest forehead out of Ant and Dec. There is no underestimating how central this brewed beverage is to the British way of life. Opening up doorways into conversations, the slurps of a good cuppa delight the ears of anyone struggling in that awkward pause between topics.

Volunteering as tea maker gives you the ability to remove yourself from any awkward British situation that may ensue.

Every day 120,000,000 cups are drunk in the UK, whilst **'Fancy a cuppa?'** and **'I'll put the kettle on'** must be two of the nation's most spoken phrases. If you stacked every box of tea sold in the UK each year on top of one another, then you will have done an incredibly stupid thing, and will most likely be arrested.

Tea is the universal lubricant that prevents our great nation from grinding to a halt – without it one is sure the British would most certainly have lost both world wars. It's a little known fact that the reason it took thirty-five years to build St Paul's Cathedral is because the work-force stopped for a tea break every five minutes.

Tea is good for you in hot weather as it raises the skin temperature to make you perspire, which in turn creates a cooling effect – not that it's that relevant in Great Britain, with our sodding weather.

The British are born with a natural instinct that allows them to make a cup of tea without ever having seen one made before. When preparing tea, there are rituals to be observed: use boiling water and, if you must resort to tea bags, always add the milk last. Failure to do so will result in such distress that it may take another cup of tea to calm everyone down again. British drinkers are required by law to utter the word 'Lovely' immediately after taking the first sip of a cup of tea. Drinking tea out of anything other than a china cup is an act of blasphemy, recognised across every faith known to mankind.

How to Make the Perfect Cup of Tea

1 Ask your maid or servant to make it for you.

2 Failing that, make it yourself you lazy sod.

3 The little finger should be raised whilst lifting the teacup – one should stress this is not for effect, but for balance.

ROYAL MAIL

Royal Mail is a fully privatised, fully bewildered, mail-delivery company whose aim is to lose half of the parcels and letters sent in the world, delivering the other half late to the wrong addresses. They have 150,000 staff, with 50 per cent of those now being given involuntary retirement. On the up side, the affected staff are being informed by letter, so they won't know about it for at least a couple of months.

Due to the increase of email, Royal Mail's prime source of business is delivering the notes telling you that they tried to deliver a package earlier in the day.

 Considering replacing Royal Mail with Usain Bolt.

Every so often, because of unfair working conditions, postal workers regularly hold national strikes – though nobody ever seems to notice. One has written many letters to Royal Mail complaining about their service, but it seems they haven't received them yet.

BRITISH SENSE OF HUMOUR

Where would we be without a good sense of humour?

Germany.

Britain's **distinctive humour** is one of the nation's defining features. When others don't get it, it's never that the joke itself wasn't funny, rather that it just sailed over the head of the person we're talking to.

British humour is the greatest of all forms of entertainment. We learn it naturally, and no other country has been able to understand us. This is particularly true with inhabitants of the USA. The difference between British humour and American humour is said to be complex, though one rather thinks it's simpler than that. There is one key difference: British humour is funny.

Britons love bleak, endlessly self-deprecating humour. The ability to laugh at ourselves during times of turmoil, tragedy and the wrong type of snow is what keeps us going when things are at their darkest; which is generally during an August bank holiday. That's why all the London hire bikes are branded with the name of a bank that was investigated for fixing interest rates. It's *supposed* to be funny.

Comedy is so important in Britain that it goes right to the heart of government. One once asked David Cameron what his favourite joke was and he said 'Nick Clegg'.

The essential ingredients of British humour can be broken down thus:

IRONY

Irony is using words to express something completely different from the literal meaning. Usually, someone says the opposite of what they mean and the listener believes the opposite of what they said. This form of humour was invented to give ourselves enough time to run away before the victim realised they'd been insulted.

SARCASM

Sarcasm is often seen as the lowest form of wit, though one can officially confirm that the lowest form of wit is actually Frankie Boyle, and that's not being sarcastic.

SELF-DEPRECATION

Self-deprecation is a form of humour
unknown to the Americans. It is when a
person says something about themselves
that is nearly always true and horrible. It
only works well when combined with
sarcasm. For example, one might make a joke
about never becoming king ... actually, let's
not go there.

SEXUAL INNUENDO

Sexual innuendo is a hard topic to stay on top
of. As a humour tool, it stands erect in the
English language, with full penetration of the
subject requiring the reader to take a hard look at
the target in order to avoid limp phrases. Some
regard it as an art form that needs a certain level
of oral skills in order for it to succeed.

THE PUN

The **pun** is a form of wordplay created by
exploiting multiple meanings of words.

TOILET HUMOUR

Toilet humour should be avoided at all times, mainly because it's shit. No pun intended.

NOTABLE BRITONS

Some are born great, some achieve greatness and some have greatness thrust upon them. And then there are those whose 'greatness' owes more to a recent appearance on *Piers Morgan's Life Stories* – otherwise Sir Bruce Forsyth* would've been forgotten years ago.

---

* The knighthood of Sir Bruce Forsyth was purely accidental. Mother stumbled whilst swinging her sword above his head and inadvertently bestowed him with his acclaimed Brucie bonus. Nice to see him, not to see him, nicer. This also happened with his previous honours, the OBE and the CBE, but you don't get anything for a pair, not in this game.

The Best of British

Helping Great Britain rule land, sea and air, here are the nation's finest sons and daughters of culture:

Charles Darwin – naturalist best known for his evolution from monkey to man, a theory which has been proved wrong by the *Jeremy Kyle Show* since 2005.

David Beckham – worldwide celebrity who was occasionally seen on a football pitch when he wasn't modeling underwear or sporting an injury. Apart from his wife, no one has ever seen if his balls are actually golden.

Agatha Christie – crime novelist whose books normally have a killer start to them.

John Lennon – musician who wrote a song detailing a world living together in peace and harmony. Imagine that. He famously outraged the United States of America by proclaiming

233

The Beatles to being 'bigger than Jesus', which effectively was true, as most people know Christ stood at 5'4".

Stephen Fry – actor, comedian, writer, Prince of Twitter and universal genius.

Helen Mirren – Mother's entertainment equivalent.

Bono – Only joking. He was actually born in the Republic of Ireland, so he's their problem now. Camilla says the difference between God and Bono is that God doesn't walk around Dublin thinking he's Bono.

Charlie Chaplin – actor, writer, director, unflagging womaniser and noted inventor of the moustache that would be responsible for one of the most destructive wars in all human history. Born into desperate poverty and the workhouse, Chaplin went to America to become the highest paid superstar in the world, but retained his manners so was kicked back out again.

Brucie bonus. Nice to see him, not to see him, nicer. This also happened with his previous honours, the OBE and the CBE, but you don't get anything for a pair, not in this game.

BRITISH COUNTRYSIDE

The British have always had a romantic view of their own **countryside**. Great Britain's idyllic green and pleasant land is as precious as any of our great cathedrals, and we erode it at our peril. Apart from Swindon – one had the dodgiest lunch there and ended up sitting on the wrong kind of throne for hours.

Rambling is one of Britain's favourite weekend pastimes. Vast herds can be seen struggling across the countryside on a Sunday morning, often identified by matching anoraks, scarves and bobble hats, in colours never before combined.

HOW TO BE TYPICALLY BRITISH

In order to be mistaken for a typical Briton, you must first master the **art of drinking so much alcohol** that you can't remember your own name. This is important, as most British pastimes involve drinking until you can't piss straight.

Should you ever be complimented on any item of clothing you are wearing, **you must say that you bought it 'in the sale'**, whether you did or didn't.

Never date. Ask a British person for a date and they are more likely to hand you a dried fruit. British people do not date. They court/pull. The British method of coupling is as follows: go to a party, get extremely drunk, kiss someone you have been making eyes at for some time but obviously have never spoken to because you were sober, go home with them, move in with them the next day, marry them. This advice is precisely based on the life story of William and Kate.

Moan about the weather at all times, even whilst sleeping. The British summer will be the most difficult time to complain, not knowing whether it's too warm or too cold. Thankfully it's normally over after a week. Don't forget to mention the hosepipe ban.

The most striking physical feature of a Brit is his or her **stiff upper lip**. British people inherit this naturally, but anyone else will need the help of liquid nitrogen. Apply the nitrogen liberally on to the upper lip, be careful not to spill it on to the teeth as you might acci*dentally* bleach them an unhealthy shade of white, thus ending any chances of being accepted into British society.

CONCLUSION

Ladies and gentlemen, please rise for the national anthem.

Don't panic, there's no need to get up really, as one understands most subjects don't know the words after the first verse.

It has been an absolute privilege guiding you all through the well-oiled workings of our green and pleasant land. As one was writing, one has had several texts and missed calls from various foreign people/Z-list celebrities asking to be the next entrants into Great Britain. Slightly confused how they ended up with one's number, but hopefully pretending to be one's voicemail message was convincing.

Right, after all this advice, one's bloody famished. Someone put the kettle on and get a bacon sandwich on the go.

ONE'S MISSION STATEMENT — CORONATION SPEECH

Anyone caught reading the following document without His Royal Highness's permission will spend the rest of their days cleaning the Tower of London with a toothbrush.

My Lords, Ladies and Gentlemen

After years of patiently waiting and endless viewings of The Lion King, one is honoured to finally be able to speak to you as your reigning monarch.

The odds of winning the EuroMillions jackpot are 1 in 116,531,800, which is currently better than the chances of finding a job under the British Government. Therefore, one has decided to dissolve Parliament and introduce legislation to make it illegal to form a government thereafter.

It seems the only way forward out of this mess is to take the bull by the horns and reintroduce absolute monarchy. The future's bright, the future's royal. One will be in charge of the environment, whilst Prince Philip will be the ideal candidate to organise foreign relations.

The Queen Mother used to say that the European Union is about as useful as tits on a nun. She was right. They want to create a unification of Europe, with Germany in charge. Brilliant plan, why hasn't anyone thought of this before? The UK will be withdrawn from the EU and the Eurovision Song Contest with immediate effect.

Independence of the United States of America will be revoked. They've had long enough to prove they can cope without royal intervention. There is no such language as US English. One will let Microsoft know about the reinstated letter 'u' and the elimination of –ize. The Fourth of July will no longer be known as Independence Day. It will

now be known as UK – Can't be Arsed Day.
Americans will no longer be allowed to own guns or
carry anything more dangerous than a potato
peeler, which will require a licence. One can
confirm that tax collectors will be with them shortly
to ensure the acquisition of all revenues due
(backdated to 1776).

Mondays will be cancelled for health and safety
reasons.

The national anthem will be on rotation every
month, with a poll deciding which song will be the
anthem for that month. To start it off, one will be
using 'We Will Rock You' by Queen. One is also
currently negotiating the beatification of Freddie
Mercury with the Roman Catholic Church. It's
exactly what Queen Elizabeth II, God rest her
soul, would've wanted.

With immediate effect it shall be illegal to be or
impersonate the following persons in public or
private:

- Sir Paul McCartney

- Justin Bieber

- Simon Cowell

- One Direction

- England football team

- Andy Murray

- David Cameron

- Nick Clegg

- George Osborne

- Members of Parliament

- Vladimir Putin

One's Mission Statement

There will be a new process for acquiring British Citizenship, where an intense set of questions will be presented to you:

1 Who is the patron saint of England?

  a) David Beckham

  b) Stephen Fry

  c) Richard Hammond

  d) St George

  e) Phillip Schofield

2 What should be done if Justin Bieber is seen on the streets of Britain?

3 How do you make your cup of tea, milk or water first?

4 Describe the relationship between you and your mother.

5 Someone stands on your foot whilst queueing at Morrisons. Should you:

a) Apologise

b) Demand an apology

c) Ignore it

d) Punch them in the face

6 Who played oneself in the Danny Boyle film, Becoming King:

a) George Clooney

b) Tom Cruise

c) Michael Sheen

d) King Charles played himself

e) None of the above

7 Marmite, love it or hate it?

8 Name at least 45 songs by The Beatles.

9 Are Cliff Richard and Mick Jagger actually twins separated at birth?

10 Red or brown sauce?

Above 95 per cent pass rate — you have the determination, courage and intelligence that one likes to see in British subjects. With your help, as well as advice from the brightest minds of this great land, we can create a country that works together. Welcome to Great Britain!

Below 95 per cent — hang your head in shame and leave the country immediately. Either you have been binge drinking or you are French in disguise.

You probably don't even know the correct pronunciation of 'water' or the names of the Spice Girls. One suggests you rehydrate yourself with plenty of English tea and study Prince @Charles_HRH's Guide to Great Britishness thoroughly from cover to cover.

Your Glorious Leader and King
Charles

ROYAL ACKNOWLEDGEMENTS

One would like to thank one's literary agent, Dame Ariella Feiner at United Agents for giving one the opportunity to write something other than books on Gardening, shopping lists, and letters to various figureheads such as Pope Francis and Father Christmas. One would also like to thank Sir Richard Roper and everyone at Headline Publishing Group for making this possible.

But, none of this would have been possible without the blessing of one's fans, followers, and future subjects.

Thank you all.

Twitter.com/Charles_HRH
Facebook.com/CharlesHRH
www.charles-hrh.com